Action!
A Parable Drama Study for Tweens

Abingdon Press
Nashville

Action!
A Parable Drama Study For Tweens

Copyright © 2009 by Abingdon Press

All rights reserved.

For information concerning permission to reproduce any material in this publication, write to Rights and Permissions, The United Methodist Publishing House, 201 Eighth Avenue, South, P.O. Box 801, Nashville, TN 37202-0801. You may fax your request to 615-749-6128, or e-mail *permissions@umpublishing.org*.

Scripture quotations in this publication, unless otherwise indicated, are from the New Revised Standard Version of the Bible, copyright 1989, Division of Christian Education of the National Council of the Churches of Christ in the United States of America. Used by permission. All rights reserved.

ISBN: 978-0-687-65601-1

Written by Nate Lee and Marcia Stoner

Cover design by Phillip D. Francis

Art Credits—pp. 44 (turbans), 45 (tunic pattern), 46 (girdles):
Teaching Tips for Terrified Teachers, © 1998 Abingdon, pp. 31, 33, 34;
pp. 45 (helmet pattern), 46 (club), 47 (clay lamp, ears), 49 (sword): Randy Wollenmann

09 10 11 12 13 14 15 16 17 18—10 9 8 7 6 5 4 3 2 1

PACP00410475-01

Manufactured in the United States of America

Contents

How to Use This Book 4

Study Sessions 5
  Parables of the Lost 6
  The Unforgiving Servant 13
  The Good Samaritan 19
  Parable of the Talents 24
  Laborers in the Vineyard 30
  The Ten Bridesmaids 36

Costumes, Props, Scenery 42

Dramas 52
  Parables of the Lost 53
  The Unforgiving Servant 62
  The Good Samaritan 68
  Parable of the Talents 75
  Laborers in the Vineyard 84
  The Ten Bridesmaids 90

How to Use This Book

Six-week Study Session on the Parables: Do the basic sessions, using the drama as the Bible portion of the study. You do not need to make costumes, props, or scenery if you are not presenting the drama as a production.

Study Retreat: May do as a retreat using two or more of the sessions. Do the basic sessions using the drama as the Bible portion of the study. You may wish to make costumes, props, and/or scenery for one of the dramas and present it at the end of the retreat or to a group after the retreat. Will not have time to learn all parts in a short retreat. They may have to do drama with scripts in hand.

Drama Camp or Tween VBS: Choose one of the dramas and prepare a full-blown production to present to the church or other group. Lead tweens through making costumes, props, and scenery. Have rehearsals, and have tweens memorize lines so that the drama may be presented in the most professional manner possible. Work with lighting and with entrances and exits to the stage.

One-time Study: Want something for a special event study? Choose one of the dramas and do the study session for that drama, using the drama itself as the Bible portion of the study. It is not necessary to make costumes, props, or scenery.

Study Sessions

Parables of the Lost

Luke 15:1-32

Scripture Verse: Luke 15:10

Faith Point: We are called to repent, and when we do, God rejoices.

The parables of the lost sheep, the lost coin, and the prodigal son all have the same message. God actively seeks out those who have sinned and are lost to the kingdom of heaven. God wants us all to repent of our sins and be open to receiving God's grace. It may seem unfair to the righteous who may feel they deserve more of God's attention, but God knows the righteous have already received grace. It is the lost who need God's help.

Supplies:
- ❏ Bibles
- ❏ photocopies of Reproducibles 1 and 2
- ❏ photocopies of pages 53-61
- ❏ small button
- ❏ highlighters
- ❏ paper
- ❏ pencils, pens, markers
- ❏ index cards
- ❏ candle and lighter
- ❏ Optional: supplies as needed for making costumes, props, scenery (pp. 42-51)

First Arrivers

Seek the Lost
- Before tweens arrive, hide a small button (or other small object) in a spot where it will be difficult to find.
- As they arrive ask tweens to hunt for the object. If they find it, they are not to pick it up or tell the others, but they are to whisper to you where they found it.
- Ask last person who finds the button to pick it up and bring it to you.

ASK: Have you ever lost anything really important to you? What did you do? Did you ever find it? If you found it, what did you do with it? If you didn't find it, what happened?

Option: Begin Costumes, Props, and Scenery
- If you are going to perform this drama publically, see pages 53-61 for the drama.
- See pages 42-51 for general instructions on costumes, props, and scenery.
- Begin these projects now. It will take time to do this and can't be done within limited time of one study session.

Prepare for Drama
Character Information
- Make and hand out copies of **Reproducible 1** (p. 11).
- Together go over character information.

Option: Read Bible
Note: You will definitely want to do this if you will be producing the drama.
- Read together Luke 15:1-32 directly from the Bible.
- Then go over character information on **Reproducible 1** (p. 11).

Drama
Before the session, photocopy "Parables of the Lost" (pp. 53-61).

Assign and Mark Parts
- Hand out copies of the drama to all tweens.
- Ask for volunteers for the parts.
- Many groups will not have enough tweens for each part, so assign more than one part to those who have smaller parts (or to everyone if necessary).
- Give everyone a highlighter and have them highlight their parts. To actors with more than one part give two or three different color highlighters so they can highlight each part in a different color.

Set Up Drama
Whether you are just going to do a walk-through reading of the drama as the Bible portion of a short-term study or you are going to produce the play for a public event, you will need to walk through the stage directions.

- Designate an area of the room as the "stage area."
- For a walk-through or for rehearsal, set up chairs and use common objects for props.
- Have tweens practice where to stand and what actions to take during drama. Let them use pencils to make notes on their scripts.

Note: Do full set-up activity even for a classroom setting. It will make drama reading go more smoothly.

Read or Rehearse Drama
If you are doing this for a study session, now is the time for tweens to read the drama, walking through it as staged. If you are going to perform the drama, run through the drama and block out staging.

Option: Rehearsal and Performance Scheduling
Before the first meeting, check with church calendar and/or any other venue in which the drama will be performed and schedule a performance date.
> **Note:** If you are going to perform elsewhere, remember that any time you transport children you need written permission of a parent or guardian.

- Hand out two photocopies per tween of **Reproducible 2** (p. 12).
- Have tweens fill in dates for rehearsals and performance on their sheet.
- Have tweens take their sheets home to give to parents (one to return and one to be posted at home).

Connect It Up

Connect the parables of the lost with your tweens' lives.

It's a Sin Challenge
- Define sin.

> **SAY:** A sin is something that separates us from God. That is, it is something that tears down our relationship with God. For example, bullying someone is a sin because we are all created by God. God wants us to treat each other with respect. Bullying is disrespectful of the person and God. Running in the halls at school may be against the rules, but it is not a sin.

- Divide tweens into small groups.
- Explain that they are to come up with a list of sins that people their age might be tempted to commit.
- Challenge them to see which group can come up with the longest list in five minutes.
- After five minutes bring groups back together and go over their lists.

> **SAY:** The prodigal son repented and asked for forgiveness. He was forgiven and given another chance.

> **ASK:** Truly repenting means changing our ways. How could people who have committed one of the sins we've listed change their ways?

- Go over as many sins as time allows, asking tweens for suggestions on how a person could change. For example, a bully could apologize for his/her behavior and in the future always speak politely to the person he/she has bullied.

Hide and Seek
- Play an old-fashioned game of hide and seek. Tweens will know the rules to this game.

   ASK: Have you ever hidden from someone or something and not wanted to be found?

   SAY: Sometimes like a sheep who is lost we want to be found. But there are many times in our lives when we are like a lost coin. We don't know we are lost.

   SAY: It's like that with the kingdom of heaven. We often hide from it because we want to be part of the crowd, and that can mean making fun of someone or trying a cigarette because it's easier than saying no. Sometimes we enjoy being mean to someone, and being part of the kingdom of heaven means we would have to change our ways.

   ASK: What do you think God does when we try to hide? *(God keeps sending help in the form of parents, teachers, the Bible, and so forth.)*

I Repent Tag
- This is a game of "gather up" tag. Some tweens may be familiar with it.
- Choose one person to be IT.
- IT tries to tag one person.
- When IT tags a person, that person joins hands with IT. These two together become IT.
- The IT team of two tries to tag someone else. When a person is tagged, that person joins hands with the other two and becomes part of IT, and so forth.
- Continue playing until all have been tagged.

   SAY: God's grace is like IT in this "gather up" tag game. We try to avoid it by continuing to do the things we want to do without regard to what God's will is for our lives. But God does not leave us alone. God will try to find us and give us grace no matter how long we run away. We can always repent of our sins and receive God's grace.

Worship

Prepare for Worship
- Give each tween an index card or a scrap piece of paper and a pen or pencil.
- Ask each to write one thing on their card or paper for which they want to repent. Assure them that nobody will read it.
- Write out one for yourself.
- Ask everyone to bring their cards/papers to worship.

Worship
- Ask a volunteer to light a candle.
- Ask another volunteer to read Luke 15:10.
- Give tweens each a marker and ask them to mark over the words on their cards/papers so they cannot be read.
- Ask tweens to tear their papers into four or five pieces.
- Instruct tweens to work together to spell the word *grace* from their torn pieces of paper on the worship table. Be sure your paper is included. (The side that has not been written on is to be face-up.)

> **PRAY:** God, Jesus has told us of your power and your grace. We were lost, but we repent of the sins that we have written today. By repenting, we open our hearts to your grace. For this we are thankful. In Jesus' name we pray. Amen.

- Ask a volunteer to blow out the candle.

Reproducible 1

Pharisees: A group of Jewish men very educated about Jewish law. They helped interpret ancient Hebrew law for their "modern" society. They felt that Jesus was not observing the religious laws and that he would cause the Romans to crush the Jewish community.

Scribes: Educated men who sometimes drew up legal documents and often advised leaders. (They really weren't secretaries, though they were responsible for preserving Scripture.)

Jesus: Often taught in parables. Parables are stories that are told to make a point.

Shepherd: Men with responsibility for all the sheep.

Woman: She was poor, and the loss of a coin was serious.

Father: A wealthy farmer who loved both sons. The father represents our heavenly father who appreciates the older son but rejoices over the saving of the younger son.

Older Son: A good man who lives a good life, but he is jealous and angry because he always did the right thing and yet the father makes a fuss over the sinful younger brother.

Younger (Prodigal) Son: A sinner, lazy, wanting everything right now and wanting to try everything—even when he knows it's bad for him. In the end, he repents and tries to turn his life around.

Merchants: Provide lots of things for people to buy.

Gambler and Wine Merchant: Represent temptation to look for pleasure instead of the kingdom of heaven.

Pig Farmer: Gives younger son way of making a living, but treats his pigs better than the young man. He represents how far the young man has fallen.

Pig: Animal that eats a lot, wallows in mud to keep cool, and doesn't really talk.

Servants: They work for the father. We don't know how they felt.

Reproducible 2

Rehearsal Schedule:

First Rehearsal _____
 (date)

Second Rehearsal _____
 (date)

Third Rehearsal _____
 (date)

Dress Rehearsal _____
 (date)

PERFORMANCE DATE: _____
 (date)

I understand that _____ is committing to attend
 (actor's name)

at least two rehearsals, plus the dress rehearsal and the performance.

_____   _____
 (signature of parent or guardian)   (date signed)

The Unforgiving Servant

Matthew 18:21-35

Scripture Verse: Colossians 3:13

Faith Point: As God forgives us we are expected to forgive others.

The parable of the unforgiving servant is about forgiveness. We all want to be forgiven, but we are often unwilling to forgive ourselves. For Christians, though, forgiveness is not an option. It's a requirement. God loves us and forgives us. Therefore we should follow this example and forgive those who have wronged us.

Supplies:
- ❑ Bibles
- ❑ photocopies of Reproducibles 2 and 3
- ❑ photocopies of pages 62-67
- ❑ prepared alphabet cards
- ❑ colored markers
- ❑ highlighters
- ❑ paper, index cards
- ❑ pencils or pens
- ❑ beanbags or small balls
- ❑ balloons
- ❑ candle and lighter
- ❑ Optional: supplies as needed for making costumes, props, scenery (pp. 42-51)

First Arrivers

Alphabet Unscramble
- Before tweens arrive, write each letter below on a separate index card, using a different color for each group of letters:
  - group one: A, B, J, P, Q, U
  - group two: C, D, K, L, S, W, X
  - group three: E, F, G, I, O, R, V
  - group four: H, M, N, T, Y, Z
- Place letters in alphabetical order on a table.
- As tweens arrive explain that they are to look for a word hidden in the alphabet. The letters of the word are scrambled.
- After a few minutes tell them that the letters to the word are all the same color. Let them pull letters out and try to make words.
- If necessary, tell them the color of the letters for the hidden word (group three). (Answer: FORGIVE)

SAY: Today we are going to learn how important it is to forgive.

Option: Begin Costumes, Props, and Scenery
- If you are going to perform this drama publically, see pages 62-67 for the drama.
- See pages 42-51 for general instructions on costumes, props, and scenery.
- Begin these projects now. It will take time to do this and can't be done within limited time of one study session.

Prepare for Drama
Character Information
- Make and hand out copies of **Reproducible 3** (p. 18).
- Together go over character information.

Option: Read Bible
Note: You will definitely want to do this if you will be producing the drama.
- Read together Matthew 18:21-35 directly from the Bible.
- Then go over character information on **Reproducible 3** (p. 18).

Drama
Before the session, photocopy "The Unforgiving Servant" (pp. 62-67).

Assign and Mark Parts
- Hand out copies of the drama to all tweens.
- Ask for volunteers for the parts.
- Many groups will not have enough tweens for each part, so assign more than one part to those who have smaller parts (or to everyone if necessary).
- Give everyone a highlighter and have them highlight their parts. To actors with more than one part give two or three different color highlighters so they can highlight each part in a different color.

Set Up Drama
Whether you are just going to do a walk-through reading of the drama as the Bible portion of a short-term study or you are going to produce the play for a public event, you will need to walk through the stage directions.

- Designate an area of the room as the "stage area."
- For a walk-through or for rehearsal, set up chairs and use common objects for props.
- Have tweens practice where to stand and what actions to take during drama. Let them use pencils to make notes on their scripts.

Note: Do full set-up activity even for a classroom setting. It will make drama reading go more smoothly.

Read or Rehearse Drama
If you are doing this for a study session, now is the time for tweens to read the drama, walking through it as staged. If you are going to perform the drama, run through the drama and block out staging.

Option: Rehearsal and Performance Scheduling
Before the first meeting, check with church calendar and/or any other venue in which the drama will be performed and schedule a performance date.
> **Note:** If you are going to perform elsewhere, remember that any time you transport children you need written permission of a parent or guardian.

- Hand out two photocopies per tween of **Reproducible 2** (p. 12).
- Have tweens fill in dates for rehearsals and performance on their sheet.
- Have tweens take their sheets home to give to parents (one to return and one to be posted at home).

Connect It Up
Connect the parable with your tweens' lives.

"Toss the Word" Bible Verse
Essentially, the Bible verse is a summary of today's message.
- Before the session, write each word (or two words) of the Bible verse on a separate piece of paper. Tape each word (or couple of words) to a small ball, beanbag, or object easily tossed.
- Have tweens sit in a circle.
- Read Colossians 3:13.
- Before beginning, practice tossing in correct pattern. Each person will toss their ball to the same person each time, so a rhythm needs to be established. Everyone must be included. Last person tosses to the first person.
- Give the first tween the first ball (words must be tossed in order).
- First person says the word (or words) and tosses the ball to the second person in the pattern established above. The second person says the word (or words) and tosses the ball.
- When first ball is halfway around, start the second ball.
- Keep adding balls. This will soon develop into chaos, but that's okay.
- When it has gotten too complicated, stop play and read the verse from the Bible.
- Read it again phrase by phrase with tweens repeating it after you.

> **ASK:** Why do you think it is so important to forgive people who have done things that hurt us? *(Forgiveness helps the person doing the forgiving. Holding onto anger is destructive.)*

"How Hard Is It?" Vote
Acknowledge that forgiving someone is not always easy.
- Give each tween five sheets of paper and a marker.
- Ask them to write these five things on their papers (one per paper) as large as possible: EASY; A LITTLE HARD; HARD; VERY HARD; REALLY, REALLY HARD.
- Explain that these will be their voting cards.
- Read each situation below. After each situation, they are to vote on how hard it would be to forgive by holding up one of their papers.
- After each vote ask why they voted that way.

SITUATION 1: Your friend asked you to help him cheat on a test. You did. You got caught. Now you're on suspension.
SITUATION 2: Your best friend told a secret about you that you didn't want anyone else to know.
SITUATION 3: Your dad promised to be at your ball game, but he got busy and forgot.
SITUATION 4: Your friend spilled a soft drink on your MP3 player and now it doesn't work. Your mother says she doesn't have money for a new one.
SITUATION 5: Someone stole $10 from your wallet. You found out who did it.

- Read Colossians 3:13.

SAY: We are asked to forgive those who have wronged us. And we are to ask for forgiveness when we have wronged others. That doesn't mean there are no consequences. Just the opposite. If someone has cheated, lied, stolen, and so forth, they must pay the consequences, but we are not to hold revenge or hatred in our hearts. We are to forgive.

"I Forgive" Balloon Bounce
Have fun acknowledging that forgiving is difficult.
- Before the session prepare three to four extra balloons as below.
- Give tweens each a balloon to blow up.
- Give everyone a marker and ask each to write "I Forgive" on the balloon after blowing it up.
- Explain that to demonstrate how difficult it can be to keep forgiving people, they have to work together to keep all the balloons in the air for five minutes. Every time a balloon hits the floor, the entire group gets five points. Explain that the goal is to get zero points. If they accumulate fifty points, they have lost.
- Have them start tossing their balloons in the air. Add the extras prepared earlier. Keep track of points.
- See how many points they have accumulated as a group. Have them grade the group effort on a scale of one to ten.

ASK: Did you get tired trying to keep the balloons in the air? Do you ever get tired of being the one who has to forgive?

SAY: When you are growing tired of forgiving people, remember that when you mess up and ask for forgiveness, God forgives you.

- Read Colossians 3:13 again.

Worship

Prepare for Worship
- Give each tween an index card or a scrap piece of paper and a pen or pencil.
- Ask each to write one thing on their card or paper for which they need to ask for forgiveness. Assure them that nobody will read this card.
- Write out a card or paper for yourself.
- Ask everyone to fold their index card or paper in half and bring it to worship.

Worship
- Ask a volunteer to light a candle.
- Explain that after the Bible reading you will model what they are to do next.
- Ask another volunteer to read Colossians 3:13.
- Ask for the paper or card from the tween on your right. Without looking at the card, tear it up and throw it in a recycling container or wastebasket.
- Ask the tween whose card you tore up to do the same thing with the person on his or her right.
- Repeat until all papers have been torn up.
- The last tween will tear up your paper.

PRAY: God, Jesus has told us of your power and your grace. We were lost, but we repent of the sins that we have written today. We ask for forgiveness and pray for the strength to not repeat any sin. In Jesus' name we pray. Amen.

SAY: In Jesus' name your sins are forgiven.

- Ask a volunteer to blow out the candle.

Peter, Andrew, John, Bartholomew: Four of Jesus' disciples. They don't really understand the kingdom of God, so they want Jesus to explain.

Jesus: Often taught in parables. Parables are stories that are told to make a point.

King: Owed money by his servants. He forgave the debt of one servant, but changed his mind after hearing the report of the servant mistreating another servant.

Accountant: Person who keeps the books. Sees everything.

Servants One and Two: Employees of the king. They probably owed money to the king because of mismanagement of funds that were their responsibility.

Unforgiving Servant: Same as Servants One and Two, but he owed about what he would earn in fifteen years. He also was owed money by the poor servant. He must have had a much higher position than the poor servant.

Poor Servant: Owed a small amount of money to the unforgiving servant.

Two Guards: Soldiers who were the king's guards. Their job was to do the bidding of the king.

The Good Samaritan

Luke 10:25-37

Scripture Verse: Matthew 5:7

Faith Point: Jesus calls us to love others and show mercy.

This story is about the importance of mercy. While those who passed by the injured man on the road probably felt mercy on him, they didn't show mercy. The Samaritan, the unexpected one, was the good neighbor because he showed mercy. We are to go and do likewise. That sometimes means being uncomfortable.

Supplies:
- Bibles
- photocopies of Reproducibles 2 and 4
- photocopies of pages 68-74
- highlighters
- pencils or pens
- large sheets of paper and/or markerboard, markers, and eraser
- beanbags, sticky balls, or darts with suction-cup tips
- paper, scissors, tape
- posterboard, markers, and craft supplies
- candle and lighter
- Optional: supplies as needed for making costumes, props, scenery (pp. 42-51)

First Arrivers

"Guess the Word" Game
Introduce some of today's concepts by playing a word guessing game.
- On a markerboard (or paper) draw one line for each letter of the chosen word or phrase.
- Players are to take turns guessing consonants.
- If a consonant is guessed correctly, write every instance of that consonant on the correct line(s).
- If a consonant is guessed correctly, then the guesser has earned the right to guess a vowel. Keep track of incorrectly guessed letters.

Game words: neighbor, merciful, help, caring, blessed, good Samaritan, friend, love, generous. Phrase: Go and do likewise. (Or use Bible verse.)

Option: Begin Costumes, Props, and Scenery
- If you are going to perform this drama publically, see pages 68-74 for the drama.
- See pages 42-51 for general instructions on costumes, props, and scenery.
- Begin these projects now. It will take time to do this and can't be done within limited time of one study session.

Prepare for Drama

Character Information
- Make and hand out copies of **Reproducible 4** (p. 23).
- Together go over character information.

Option: Read Bible
Note: You will definitely want to do this if you will be producing the drama.
- Read together Luke 10:25-37 directly from the Bible.
- Then go over character information on **Reproducible 4** (p. 23).

Drama

Before the session, photocopy "The Good Samaritan" (pp. 68-74).

Assign and Mark Parts
- Hand out copies of the drama to all tweens.
- Ask for volunteers for the parts.
- Many groups will not have enough tweens for each part, so assign more than one part to those who have smaller parts (or to everyone if necessary).
- Give everyone a highlighter and have them highlight their parts. To actors with more than one part give two or three different color highlighters so they can highlight each part in a different color.

Set Up Drama
Whether you are just going to do a walk-through reading of the drama as the Bible portion of a short-term study or you are going to produce the play for a public event, you will need to walk through the stage directions.

- Designate an area of the room as the "stage area."
- For a walk-through or for rehearsal, set up chairs and use common objects for props.
- Have tweens practice where to stand and what actions to take during drama. Let them use pencils to make notes on their scripts.

Note: Do full set-up activity even for a classroom setting. It will make drama reading go more smoothly.

Read or Rehearse Drama
If you are doing this for a study session, now is the time for tweens to read the drama, walking through it as staged. If you are going to perform the drama, run through the drama and block out staging.

Option: Rehearsal and Performance Scheduling
Before the first meeting, check with church calendar and/or any other venue in which the drama will be performed and schedule a performance date.
> **Note:** If you are going to perform elsewhere, remember that any time you transport children you need written permission of a parent or guardian.

- Hand out two photocopies per tween of **Reproducible 2** (p. 12).
- Have tweens fill in dates for rehearsals and performance on their sheet.
- Have tweens take their sheets home to give to parents (one to return and one to be posted at home).

Connect It Up
Connect the parable with your tweens' lives.

When Do We Need Neighbors?
- Ask a volunteer to read Luke 10:36-37.
- Using a markerboard or large sheet of paper, brainstorm times when we might need a good neighbor (that is, when we might need mercy). Examples: when we're sick or lonely; when our dog dies or we fail a course in school; when someone is hungry, and so forth.
- Accept all reasonable suggestions.
- Ask a volunteer to read Matthew 5:7.

How Can You Be a Neighbor?
- Go through the list you brainstormed above.
- For each situation ask tweens to state one way they could be a neighbor (show mercy) to someone in that situation.

Target Practice
Have fun learning the Bible verse.

Before the session draw a target on a large sheet of paper and gather beanbags or some sticky balls that stick to whatever you throw them at. Darts with suction-cup tips would also work.

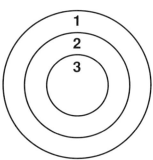

Write out the Bible verse, separating the words so that they can be cut apart. Make photocopies and then cut words apart—you'll need one cut-apart verse for each tween.

- Ask a volunteer to read Matthew 5:7.
- Explain that the object of the game is to be able to collect all the words of the Bible verse and put the verse together.
- Give each tween a turn at throwing the beanbag, ball, or other chosen object at the target.
- If a tween hits the target in any area, give him or her the number of words corresponding to the number on the target.
- Tweens rotate throwing at the target, one throw per turn.
- Give each tween the same number of chances to accumulate cards.
- Bring everyone back together and ask if they know what the word *mercy* means. *(To show mercy means to treat others with kindness and sympathy, without asking if they deserve it.)*

Worship

Prepare for Worship
- Provide a sheet of posterboard and craft supplies for every three tweens.
- Divide tweens into groups of three and have each group work together to produce a poster using today's Scripture verse (Matthew 5:7—Blessed are the merciful, for they will receive mercy.)

Worship
- Ask a volunteer to light a candle.
- Ask another volunteer to read Matthew 5:7.
- Ask each group to hang their worship poster on the wall.

> **PRAY:** God, Jesus has told us of your power and your grace. We have been shown that being merciful is your desire for us. Help us to show mercy to someone this week. In Jesus' name we pray. Amen.

- Ask a volunteer to blow out the candle.

Lawyer: Probably an expert in the Jewish law.

Jesus: Often taught in parables. Parables are stories that are told to make a point.

Man: We know nothing about this man except that he was robbed. We don't know if he was a Jew or a Gentile.

Robbers One, Two, and Three: Tough guys who robbed and beat the man. They didn't care who he was.

Priest: A priest who was probably very busy and wanted to be ritually clean. (They were not allowed to touch blood before performing religious duties.) However, no reason is given as to why the priest passed the man by. Is there ever a really good excuse?

Levite: A descendent of Levi. (Levi was one of Jacob's sons, the founder of one of the twelve tribes of Israel.) Could have held any number of religious jobs. Probably was a busy man. No reason is given as to why the Levite passed the man by. Is there ever a really good excuse?

Samaritan: A man from a Hebrew religious sect called Samaritans. Some of their beliefs were a little different than that of the other Hebrews (Jews). Samaritans and Jews did not get along well.

Innkeeper: Man who lived in the area and knew what people thought of Samaritans. He would have been surprised that a Samaritan would help a Jew.

Disciples: Jesus' followers who didn't understand everything Jesus said, so he often had to teach them in parables.

Parable of the Talents

Matthew 25:14-30

Scripture Verse: Matthew 5:16

Faith Point: As disciples of Jesus we are called to active service.

This story is about the kingdom of God and what actions Christians are to take now. To be faithful means to act now, and that includes taking the initiative ourselves and even taking some risks. Sitting around doing nothing bad is not enough. We are to act on our faith.

Supplies:
- Bibles
- photocopies of Reproducibles 2 and 5
- photocopies of pages 75-83
- balloons, hard candy
- highlighters
- matches or lighter; candles with drip guards
- Optional: supplies as needed for making costumes, props, scenery (pp. 42-51)
- Optional: cash, basket, index cards, pencils or pens (p. 27)

First Arrivers

Take Care of the Balloon(s)
Introduce the concept of risk in this opening activity.
Blow up balloons before the session. Do not tie with string.
- As tweens arrive, give each tween a balloon and explain that they will have to work on some projects.
- Then tell them that while they work on the projects they must take care of the balloon. They must keep it off the ground, and it cannot pop.
- Also explain that they will get a treat for every balloon they can take care of and still do their project.
- Then ask if anyone wants more than one balloon to take care of.
- Assign a task such as cleaning the room or working on props or scenery.
- When most have arrived bring everyone together and hand out treats (such as hard candy) for each balloon that never hit the floor.

SAY: Those who took a chance might have struggled more, but they also were taking a chance of a bigger reward. Our story today is about taking a chance for your faith.

Option: Begin Costumes, Props, and Scenery
- If you are going to perform this drama publically, see pages 75-83 for the drama.
- See pages 42-51 for general instructions on costumes, props, and scenery.
- Begin these projects now. It will take time to do this and can't be done within limited time of one study session.

Prepare for Drama

Read Bible
- Read together Matthew 25:14-30 directly from the Bible.

Character Information
- Make and hand out copies of **Reproducible 5** (p. 29).
- Together go over character information.

Drama

Before the session, photocopy "Parable of the Talents" (pp. 75-83).

Assign and Mark Parts
- Hand out copies of the drama to all tweens.
- Ask for volunteers for the parts.
- Many groups will not have enough tweens for each part, so assign more than one part to those who have smaller parts (or to everyone if necessary).
- Give everyone a highlighter and have them highlight their parts. To actors with more than one part give two or three different color highlighters so they can highlight each part in a different color.

Set Up Drama
Whether you are just going to do a walk-through reading of the drama as the Bible portion of a short-term study or you are going to produce the play for a public event, you will need to walk through the stage directions.

- Designate an area of the room as the "stage area."
- For a walk-through or for rehearsal, set up chairs and use common objects for props.
- Have tweens practice where to stand and what actions to take during drama. Let them use pencils to make notes on their scripts.

Note: Do the full set-up activity even for a classroom setting. It will make drama reading go more smoothly.

Read or Rehearse Drama
If you are doing this for a study session, now is the time for tweens to read the drama, walking through it as staged. If you are going to perform the drama, run through the drama and block out staging.

Option: Rehearsal and Performance Scheduling
Before the first meeting, check with church calendar and/or any other venue in which the drama will be performed and schedule a performance date.
>**Note:** If you are going to perform elsewhere, remember that any time you transport children you need written permission of a parent or guardian.

- Hand out two photocopies per tween of **Reproducible 2** (p. 12).
- Have tweens fill in dates for rehearsals and performance on their sheet.
- Have tweens take their sheets home to give to parents (one to return and one to be posted at home).

Connect It Up
Connect the parable with your tweens' lives.

Fruit Basket Upset With a Twist
- Before beginning, pull one tween aside and give the instruction that no matter what happens during the game, she or he is NOT to leave her or his chair during the game. (And she/he is not to tell anyone.)
- Have tweens sit in chairs in a circle with one tween designated as IT standing in the center of the circle.
- Give each tween (including IT) the name of a fruit, making sure that each fruit is represented a minimum of twice and up to four times depending upon size of group.
- IT is to stand in the middle of a circle and yell out a fruit. All those with that fruit name are to switch seats, with IT trying to get a seat.
- The one left standing becomes IT.
- If IT yells "fruit basket upset," everyone must change seats (except the one instructed not to move).
- After a few rounds ask the one who didn't move during the game what it felt like.

>**SAY:** Those who took a chance and played the game risked losing their seat. The one who didn't move always had a seat, but didn't get to play the game. That's what the parable is trying to tell us.

Faithfulness means risking something for a greater reward. Being a part of God's kingdom—really living a faithful, meaningful life—means actively living what we believe, not just thinking about it.

"Let Your Light Shine" Mimes
Explore one meaning of today's Scripture verse.

- Ask a volunteer to read Matthew 5:14-16.

    SAY: In the parable of the talents, the servants were entrusted with the master's money. They were to do something with it. They were to make the money work for the master. As Christians we are entrusted with letting the world know about God and glorifying God.

- Divide tweens into small groups (have groups of boys and groups of girls if possible).
- Ask a volunteer to read Matthew 5:16.
- Tell each group they have five minutes to decide on one way they can do good work and prepare to act it out without words.
- After five minutes bring the groups back together and let each group act out their "good work" while the other groups try to guess what they are doing.

    SAY: When we do good works and give God the glory we are letting our light shine before others and we are multiplying the number of people who feel God's love. We are being the good servants.

Optional: Multiply Your Service
Choose an important service ministry of the church to raise money for. Decide on an amount of money the church is comfortable with—$20, $50, or whatever—and divide it up into small bills as service-project seed money.

   SAY: You are going to be given a chance to be good servants and multiply your money for the Lord. I will pass a basket of money. You are to take out an amount that you feel you can multiply by using in some way. You will be asked to sign a card saying how much money you took. On _____
   (date)
   you are to bring back that amount plus the money you earned.

- Give each tween an index card and pencil and, after the basket has gone around, have them write the amount they took on the card and sign it. Explain that they may work alone, in pairs, or in small groups to choose what they will do and how they will work on their service project.

IMPORTANT: Follow through. You may not get back some of the money, but often kids will make more than you expect.

Optional: Multiply Your Service as a Discussion
If you will not be getting back together or the church prefers not to participate in an actual service project, use the same idea for an in-session activity:

Choose an important service ministry of the church to discuss. Divide the group into pairs or threes and assign each group a different amount of "money" to work with.

> **ASK:** You are being given a chance to be good servants and multiply your money for the Lord. What will you do to use the money you have to increase it?

- Give each group time to make a decision, and ask them to report on their decisions.

Worship

Prepare for Worship
- Ask tweens to brainstorm ways they can do something good this week.
- Ask each tween to choose one of these ways or one they think of on their own to commit to doing this week.
- Give each tween a small candle with drip protector (such as those used for candlelight services).
- Give instructions before worship: The candles will be lit. Tweens are each to sit with a hand cupped so that the flame can't be seen by others.
- At the appropriate time you will begin, and in turn as they are seated they will state what good thing they have committed to doing this week. As they do so they are to take their hand away and let their candle shine.

Worship
- When tweens are seated in worship area, light each candle.
- Ask another volunteer to read Matthew 5:16.

> **PRAY:** Dear God, we commit to letting our lights shine to show your glory this week. In Jesus' name we pray. Amen.

- Begin the candle activity by stating your own commitment and moving your hand away from the candle. Signal for the tween beside you to do likewise.

- Ask everyone to blow out their candles.

Reproducible 5

Jesus: Often taught in parables. Parables are stories that are told to make a point.

Disciples: Jesus' followers who didn't understand everything Jesus said, so he often had to teach them in parables.

Assistant: The person in charge of keeping Mr. Bigg's schedule and making sure things run smoothly.

Mr. Bigg: A businessman, the boss. He gives each of three of his employees a challenge. He expects results.

Mary: A servant. She has a responsible position, and Mr. Bigg puts her in charge of fifty thousand dollars. Mary is a very good manager and is willing to take chances. Mary likes to "think big."

Isaac: A servant. He has a responsible position, and Mr. Bigg puts him in charge of twenty-five thousand dollars. Isaac is a very good manager and is willing to take chances.

Jonah: A servant. He has a responsible position, and Mr. Bigg puts him in charge of five thousand dollars. Jonah is unsure of himself and doesn't want to disappoint Mr. Bigg.

A TALENT—In the drama we use dollars because that is easier for us to understand. However, the Bible uses a *talent*. A talent was a unit of money equal to about six thousand drachmas. There are differences of opinion as to how much a drachma was worth, but the exact amount is not important to the story. The story is about whether to play it safe or to step out in faith.

Laborers in the Vineyard

Matthew 20:1-16

Scripture Verse: Ephesians 2:8

Faith Point: We are saved by God's grace.

This story turns everything we believe about fairness upside down. No matter how long or how short a time the laborers work, they are all paid the same thing. We think of that as unjust. But remember, this is a parable, not an argument for changing labor laws. This parable demonstrates that we do not earn our way into God's kingdom. God's grace is offered to all, no matter how late in life they turn to God.

Supplies:
- Bibles
- photocopies of Reproducibles 2 and 6
- photocopies of pages 84-89
- treats/candy, container
- highlighters
- markerboard, markers
- deck of cards
- index cards
- pencils or pens
- candle and lighter
- Optional: supplies as needed for making costumes, props, scenery (pp. 42-51)

First Arrivers

"That's Not Fair" Task
Introduce the problem with the parable.
- As tweens arrive give them each a task to do. It should be the same task for all. For example, working on props, washing windows, or setting up the room.
- Explain that when they finish they will be given a treat.
- When all have gathered, give everyone a treat or reward. The treat is the same for everybody, no matter how late they came. If they started the task, the reward is the same.
- If tweens do not protest about unfairness, ask them if they think it is fair for everyone to get the same treat although they didn't all work for the same length of time.

ASK: If you mowed a lawn all day, would it be fair if someone who helped you for only the last hour got paid exactly the same thing?

SAY: The parable we will look at today talks about a problem like this.

Option: Divide the Candy
- Bring in a container of individually wrapped candies. Count them ahead of time. You will want the count to be unequal to number of tweens.

NOTE: Before beginning this activity, count tweens and adjust number of pieces of candy so that there will be an uneven distribution.

- Ask tweens to work together to divide up all of the candy.
- Sit back and let them work it out. Observe how they solve the problem.

ASK: Are you all happy with the amount of candy you got? Was the distribution fair? How did you decide what was fair?

SAY: Today's parable helps us understand that we can't earn our way into the kingdom of heaven.

Prepare for Drama

Read Bible
- Read together Matthew 20:1-16 directly from the Bible.

Character Information
- Make and hand out copies of **Reproducible 6** (p. 35).
- Together go over character information.

Drama

Before the session, photocopy "Laborers in the Vineyard" (pp. 84-89).

Assign and Mark Parts
- Hand out copies of the drama to all tweens.
- Ask for volunteers for the parts.
- Many groups will not have enough tweens for each part, so assign more than one part to those who have smaller parts (or to everyone if necessary).
- Give everyone a highlighter and have them highlight their parts. To actors with more than one part give two or three different color highlighters so they can highlight each part in a different color.

Set Up Drama
Whether you are just going to do a walk-through reading of the drama as the Bible portion of a short-term study or you are going to produce the play for a public event, you will need to walk through the stage directions.
- Designate an area of the room as the "stage area."
- For a walk-through or for rehearsal, set up chairs and use common objects for props.
- Have tweens practice where to stand and what actions to take during drama. Let them use pencils to make notes on their scripts.

Note: Do the full set-up activity even for a classroom setting. It will make drama reading go more smoothly.

Read or Rehearse Drama
If you are doing this for a study session, now is the time for tweens to read the drama, walking through it as staged. If you are going to perform the drama, run through the drama and block out staging.

Option: Rehearsal and Performance Scheduling
Before the first meeting, check with church calendar and/or any other venue in which the drama will be performed and schedule a performance date.
> **Note:** If you are going to perform elsewhere, remember that any time you transport children you need written permission of a parent or guardian.

- Hand out two photocopies per tween of **Reproducible 2** (p. 12).
- Have tweens fill in dates for rehearsals and performance on their sheet.
- Have tweens take their sheets home to give to parents (one to return and one to be posted at home).

Connect It Up

Connect the parable with your tweens' lives.

Note: If you did not do the "Divide the Candy" activity on page 31, you may do it at this time.

Ten Clues
- Divide tweens into two groups.
- Explain that they are to work together to figure out what word you are thinking of. You will give ten clues. The first group to guess the word wins.
- Give clues in order.

CLUES: 1. You can't hold it; 2. You can't touch it; 3. You can't smell it; 4. You can't see it; 5. You can't buy it; 6. You can't trade for it; 7. You can't earn it; 8. You can't save it up; 9. It can be given only by God; 10. It saves you. ANSWER: GRACE

SAY: Today's parable explains that we do good works because that's what faithful people do. These good works come out of our faith. However, these good works don't earn us a place in heaven. Our faith opens us up to receive the grace that comes only from God.

- Ask a volunteer to read Ephesians 2:8.

"Go Fish" for Grace
Before the session take an ordinary deck of playing cards (or a specialty set of Go Fish cards) and, using a marker (black will work best), write the word *grace* on eight to ten random cards.

- Shuffle the cards (except the GRACE cards—make sure they all end up in the "Go Fish" pile).
- Deal cards out to tweens, explaining that they will have to match four-of-a-kind sets—that is, all queens, all tens, all fours, and so forth. Most kids know the rules for Go Fish and can explain it to those who don't.
- Explain that if they get a GRACE card, it's like a wild card. They can use it to make a set of four of something, even if they have only one of that card.
- Play the game, ending when one player is out of cards.
- Ask those who got a GRACE card if it was easier to be able to lay down cards without having to save up four of a kind.
- If someone hasn't received one, ask how it felt to be left out.

SAY: God's grace makes hard times easier because we know we can turn to God and other Christians for help. We can receive grace from God at any time. God's grace is there and offered to us. We have to be open to receiving it.

Option: Give Grace Away
If time allows, play the game again. This time shuffle the GRACE cards in with the others.

Play the game as above, with the exception that a player can use only one GRACE card. If a player has or draws a second or third GRACE card, the player gives it to someone without a GRACE card.

SAY: When we invite others to church or Sunday school, when we act with kindness and understanding, when we help other people, we help them see a chance for God's grace.

Worship

Prepare for Worship

- Ask tweens to brainstorm ways they can help people see God this week.
- Ask each tween to choose one of these ways or one they think of on their own to commit to doing this week.
- Ask them to write that commitment on an index card and sign their name.
- Ask them to bring the index card to worship.
- At the appropriate time you will begin, and in turn as they are seated they will state what good thing they have committed to doing this week.

Worship
- Ask a volunteer to light a candle.
- Ask another volunteer to read Ephesians 2:8–9.
- Ask everyone to hold their commitment cards during the prayer.

PRAY: Dear God, thank you for your grace in our lives. This week each of us commits to help show your grace to others. We commit ourselves to your service. In Jesus' name we pray. Amen.

- Ask tweens to put the cards away in a pocket or purse to carry with them this week to remind them of their promises to God.

- Ask a volunteer to blow out the candle.

John: One of the disciples closest to Jesus. He is asking a question to which they all want an answer.

Other Disciples: Jesus' followers who didn't understand everything Jesus said, so he often had to teach them in parables.

Jesus: Often taught in parables. Parables are stories that are told to make a point.

Vineyard Owner: A rich man with a large vineyard. He keeps going out and hiring new people to work in his vineyard for the day. He agrees to give the first laborers the usual daily wage. He tells the others he will pay them what is right. At the end of the day he gives everyone the same amount of money. On top of that, the ones who came last he pays first.

Workers One, Two, and Three: The first workers hired. They worked hard all day and expected to be paid more than those hired later in the day. They were last in line to receive pay.

Workers Four, Five, Six, Seven and Eight: Workers hired by afternoon. They received the same amount as everyone else, but not much else is said about them.

Workers Nine, Ten, and Eleven: They were hired late in the day. They didn't work very long. They were put first in line to receive pay and were paid as much as everyone else.

Assistant: Person in charge of seeing that everyone gets paid. He just follows the vineyard owner's orders.

The Ten Bridesmaids

Matthew 25:1-13

Scripture Verse: Matthew 25:13

Faith Point: Discipleship can't be put off. A Christian must be faithful at all times.

This story is about discipleship. We are told we know neither the day nor the hour of Jesus' return, the coming of the kingdom on earth. And we're not supposed to worry about that. What we are supposed to do is to live like the kingdom is here already so that we are prepared. We are to be disciples in everything we say and do right now! No putting it off!

Supplies:
- Bibles
- photocopies of Reproducibles 2 and 7
- photocopies of pages 90-96
- pencils, pens
- paper, construction paper, posterboard
- highlighters
- old newspapers
- markers
- pushpins or tape
- candle and lighter
- Optional: supplies as needed for making costumes, props, scenery (pp. 42-51)

First Arrivers

Sit and Wait
Introduce the idea of waiting.
- After five or six tweens have arrived, assign each a place in the room to wait.
- Instruct them not to doodle, not to talk, not to do anything—just wait quietly and be ready to come together at your signal.
- As others arrive, have them do the same.
- After five minutes call them together.

> **ASK:** Did you have any idea what you were waiting for? Was it hard to wait quietly and be attentive, or did your mind wander? Did you want to do other things? Did you get sleepy? Did you get tired of waiting?

Think Up Wise and Foolish Sayings
Introduce the idea of being wise or foolish.
- Divide tweens into groups of three to five.
- Have each group select someone to record their statements.
- Ask the groups to come up with five wise sayings or wise pieces of advice. These can be things they have heard or that they make up themselves.
- After about ten minutes ask them to come up with five sayings or advice a person would be foolish to follow.
- After another five or ten minutes call everyone together.
- Ask each group to report their wise sayings/advice first.
- Then have each group report on their foolish sayings/advice.

TIP: Encourage tweens to have fun and think imaginatively with these sayings. Ask them to come up with things they think the other groups might not have thought of.

Prepare for Drama
Read Bible
- Read together Matthew 25:1-13 directly from the Bible.

Character Information
- Make and hand out copies of **Reproducible 7** (p. 41).
- Together go over character information.

Drama
Before the session, photocopy "The Ten Bridesmaids" (pp. 90-96).

Assign and Mark Parts
- Hand out copies of the drama to all tweens.
- Ask for volunteers for the parts.
- Many groups will not have enough tweens for each part, so assign more than one part to those who have smaller parts (or to everyone if necessary).
- Give everyone a highlighter and have them highlight their parts. To actors with more than one part give two or three different color highlighters so they can highlight each part in a different color.

Set Up Drama
Whether you are just going to do a walk-through reading of the drama as the Bible portion of a short-term study or you are going to produce the play for a public event, you will need to walk through the stage directions.
- Designate an area of the room as the "stage area."
- For a walk-through or for rehearsal, set up chairs and use common objects for props.

- Have tweens practice where to stand and what actions to take during drama. Let them use pencils to make notes on their scripts.

Note: Do the full set-up activity even for a classroom setting. It will make drama reading go more smoothly.

Read or Rehearse Drama
If you are doing this for a study session, now is the time for tweens to read the drama, walking through it as staged. If you are going to perform the drama, run through the drama and block out staging.

Option: Rehearsal and Performance Scheduling
Before the first meeting, check with church calendar and/or any other venue in which the drama will be performed and schedule a performance date.
> **Note:** If you are going to perform elsewhere, remember that any time you transport children you need written permission of a parent or guardian.

- Hand out two photocopies per tween of **Reproducible 2** (p. 12).
- Have tweens fill in dates for rehearsals and performance on their sheet.
- Have tweens take their sheets home to give to parents (one to return and one to be posted at home).

Connect It Up
Connect the parable with your tweens' lives.

"Pass the Light" Bible Verse Game
Today's Bible verse summarizes how a disciple is to live, so help tweens remember it.

- Have "lights" for each tween to pass. The simplest way to do this is to have small (unlit) candles that can be used later for worship. Or you can have tweens each write the word *light* or *lamp* on a piece of paper and tape it to a marker.
- Have everyone sit in a circle (or around a table).
- Read Matthew 25:13.
- Ask tweens to repeat the Bible verse after you.
- Explain that you will all say the Bible verse together. As each word is said, they will pass their "lights" to the person on their right.
- They must pass their "lights" on each word so that they are passing and receiving at the same time.
- Explain that you will start slowly.

- Practice passing and reciting the Bible verse one time. Do this very slowly.
- Begin the Bible verse again with everyone passing. Do it a little faster.
- Do this several times, getting faster each time until it becomes almost impossible to accomplish. (Passing and reciting will probably break down altogether, but by then they will probably have learned the verse.)

Note: If you did not do the "Think Up Wise and Foolish Sayings" activity on page 37, you may wish to do it at this time.

Musical Excuses Game
Make a floor game using old newspapers or construction paper.

- Push all furniture back and have tweens help make a gameboard by placing old newspaper or construction paper as "spaces" around the room in a pattern. The starting and ending "space" will be the same. Have a volunteer draw a big X on one of the "spaces."
- The tweens themselves will be the game pieces.
- Explain that you will play some music and they are to step from space to space until the music stops. Only one person can be on a space at a time.
- When you stop the music they must stop where they are.
- You will read a statement, and the person standing on the X will have to come up with an excuse for not doing it or doing something else instead. (Excuses don't actually have to match the situation.)
- Play begins again until all five statements have been read.

Statements:
1. The church has requested we give extra money to the food pantry.
2. Your mother has suggested you invite the new kid down the street to Sunday school.
3. It's time to go to church on Sunday morning.
4. You've been asked to sing in the youth choir.
5. You hurt someone's feelings and you know you should apologize.

TIP: You may wish to make up statements that specifically fit your group.

- Bring the group back together and ask a volunteer to read Matthew 25:13.

> **SAY:** It's easy to put off things we don't want to do or to do the easy thing. Besides, you're young; it's easy to think you have lots of time. However, the Bible tells us that, for Christians, discipleship means acting as if today may be the last chance we get. That means we can't use excuses to act as Christians tomorrow instead of today.

What's the Difference Between Wise and Intelligent?

Ask tweens if they know what the difference between being wise and being intelligent is.

SAY: People who are intelligent are able to process a lot of information and put it to use. However, even an intelligent person may not be wise. To be wise is to be able to understand what is true, what is right, what is the best thing to do, and what the consequences of an action will be.

Worship

Prepare for Worship
Make "wise discipleship" signs.

> **SAY:** We are asked to live wisely, being disciples and living our faith right now. Let's make some "wise discipleship" signs to post in our worship area.

- Have markers and paper, construction paper, or posterboard available. Also have available something to post signs with.
- Ask tweens each to select from the New Testament some wise advice on how to be a good disciple.

Possibly choose from these Scriptures: Matthew 5:3-11 (any of the Beatitudes), 7:12, 18:21-22 (How often should I forgive? Seventy-seven times), 25:40b (begin with "just"); Mark 4:24; Luke 6:27, 6:37, 11:28.

- Ask them to select a marker and a piece of paper, construction paper, or posterboard and to copy their chosen verse from the Bible onto their paper.
- Ask them to bring their "wise discipleship" signs to worship.

Worship
- Ask a volunteer to light a candle.
- Ask another volunteer to read Matthew 25:13.
- Ask everyone to hang their "wise discipleship" sign on the wall in the worship area.
- When finished ask each to read her or his sign aloud.

> **PRAY:** Our God, we hear your call to be wise. We will try to live each day as you want us to live, remembering you in our hearts, and following Jesus' teachings. In Jesus' name we pray. Amen.

- Ask a volunteer to blow out the candle.

Bartholomew: One of Jesus' disciples. He's having trouble understanding the kingdom of heaven, but he finds it easier to phrase it as a question from Thomas.

Peter: One of Jesus' closest disciples. He's having trouble understanding the kingdom of heaven too.

Disciples: Jesus' followers who didn't understand everything Jesus said, so he often had to teach them in parables.

Jesus: Often taught in parables. Parables are stories that are told to make a point.

Wise Bridesmaids One, Two, Three, Four, and Five: These five wedding attendants know what is expected of them, and they plan ahead so that they are able to do this. They anticipate (figure out ahead of time) what would happen if they were unprepared.

Foolish Bridesmaids One, Two, Three, Four, and Five: These five wedding attendants know what is expected of them, but they fail to plan ahead so that they are able to do this. They aren't much concerned about anything going wrong. They are more interested in their immediate enjoyment (or sleep) than they are with their duties. They then have to deal with a crisis when they have been caught unprepared.

Servant: The servant's role is to awaken the bridesmaids.

Groom: The groom at the wedding. He must hurry into the wedding (after all, the bride is waiting). He doesn't have time to wait around for the foolish bridesmaids to get their act together.

Costumes
Props
Scenery

Costumes

If you are using the dramas for study sessions only, let tweens wear their own clothes. Or you may wish to add headgear to denote different characters.

For full-blown presentations, Jesus and the disciples should be in biblical costume. The characters of the parable itself can be dressed in either biblical costume or modern clothing, depending on if you want to do the drama as a straight "biblical" story or to have a modern context for the parable parts.

Headgear

Headbands may be used for both males and females. Measure heads and cut strips of cloth about four inches longer than that so the headbands can be tied.

For some of the biblical men and women, make head wraps. A head wrap is a square piece of cloth placed on top of the head with one or both ends draped up and around the neck.

For men of higher status you can make a turban out of wrapped cloth. For a high priest, trim the turban with ribbon or cord.

Turbans

Make a cardboard crown for the king.

For bridesmaids' flowered wreaths, weave or tie together artificial flowers in a circle that will sit on the head.

Helmets for soldiers can be made using 1-gallon or 1 1/2-gallon bleach bottles. Enlarge pattern (below) and trace onto lower part of bottle (flip pattern over for other side of bottle). Cut bottle along lines, being sure to cut away the bottom part of the bottle. Sand edges and then use silver spray paint or felt-tip markers to decorate. Glue on additional decorations as desired.

Helmet Pattern

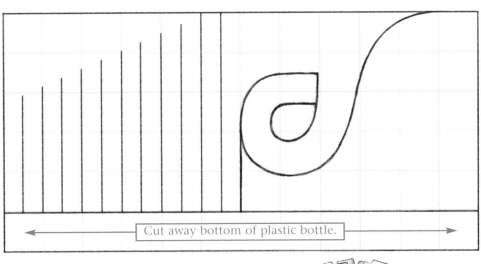

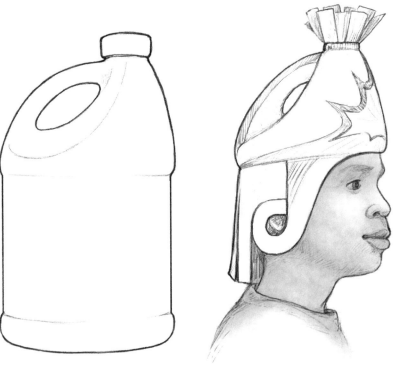

Tunics

In order for tweens to be able to make the costumes themselves, simply begin with large straight pieces of cloth. Tweens can cut out a neck opening, fold, and sew in simple stitches down the sides.

Men usually wore shorter tunics (to the knees), and women wore longer tunics.

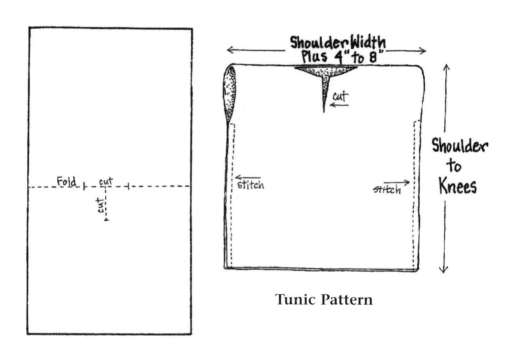

Tunic Pattern

Use different kinds of cloth to show different social status. For poor people, such as vineyard workers, use a coarse cloth. To show higher economic status use a smooth cotton or a linen.

For women and the rich, let tweens sew on braids or other trim.

Girdles

Both men and women wore large belts (girdles) wrapped around their waists with the ends hanging down. Women's should be more colorful. (See illustrations on p. 46.)

Permission is granted to reproduce this page for local church use.
This text must appear on the duplicate. © 2009 Abingdon Press

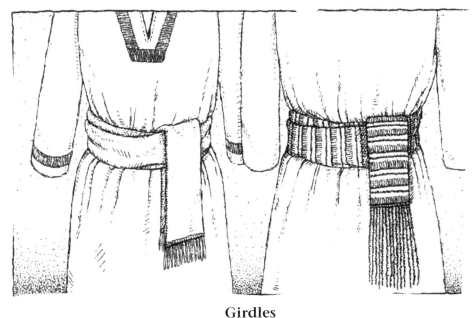
Girdles

Feet
No matter what the status, everyone wears sandals. Let everyone wear their own (the plainer the better).

Props

Clubs for Robbers
Safety is important, so have tweens roll newspapers into long cylinders and tape them closed. Then mold smaller pieces of newspaper around one end of each newspaper cylinder to make one end rounded. Paint the clubs dark brown.

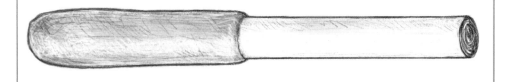

Clay Lamps

Cover work area with a plain cloth (not newspapers—newsprint rubs off).

Shape self-drying clay into a crude oil lamp. (Exact shape is not important, but biblical lamps were usually fairly low and had a handle for carrying.) Set aside on a paper plate or wax paper to dry.

It will take several days for the lamps to dry.

If you would like to use in closing worship, pour a small amount of lamp oil or olive oil into each lamp and add a piece of wick.

The wick needs to be long enough to extend over the edge of the lamp.

NOTE: Oil may seep through the clay, so set each lamp on a saucer or small plate before filling.

Ears—Donkey or Pig

Purchase a plastic headband.

Out of paper cut two ear shapes —long for a donkey, short for a pig. You may wish to begin with white paper and color the ears with shadings that make them look more "earlike."

Down the center of the back of each ear glue a chenille stick (this will allow ears to bend).

Glue ears to plastic headband. Wrap gently with masking tape to hold in place till glue is dry.

Remove masking tape.

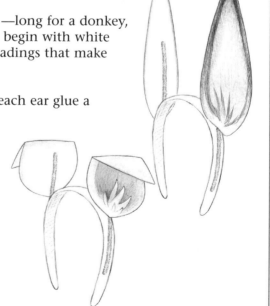

Coins
You may use real coins or make coins. To make coins, use a small round object such as a quarter or a large bottle cap as a pattern to draw circles out of posterboard. (Irregular circles are fine; biblical coins wouldn't have been perfect.) Cut out the circles. Cover each circle completely with aluminum foil.

Modern Lamps
Gather all kinds of modern lamps for the bridesmaids, such as a desk lamp, a flashlight, a lantern, and so forth, each one different.

OR

Make modern lights (extra large) by first freehand drawing the desired shape of lamp onto posterboard or cardboard. Cut out the shape. Use markers or paints to make color so that it looks like desired light.

For a fancy table lamp add braid or trim or maybe even beads.

Coin Pouch
Use a small round plate as a pattern for drawing and cutting a circle out of brown or black felt.

With a one-hole paper punch, punch holes at even intervals around the circle. (Six to eight holes should be sufficient, depending upon size.)

Lace yarn or a leather cord through the holes.

Pull yarn or cord on both ends, gathering the felt at the top. Coins can be placed in this pouch.

Signs
Use posterboard, markers, and your imagination to make signs.

Oversized Wall Clock
Cut a large circle out of a cardboard box. Paint the circle a solid color. Let dry. Paint clock face on the circle.

To turn this into a "grandfather clock," simply have a tween stand holding the clock face in front of her or his face during the performance.

Travel Bag for Good Samaritan
Cut two rectangles, the same size, out of cloth. Place one on top of the other, wrong sides together. Punch holes down both sides and across the bottom. Thread leather strips, sturdy string, or small rope through the holes. Tie off. (Do not pull strings; you want it to lie flat.) Punch a set of holes on each side of the top. Loop a long string or rope to make a shoulder handle. Tie off so it will stay put. Stuff with paper or light items to make pouch look full.

Oversized Calculator

For humorous effect, make an oversized calculator. Cut a piece of cardboard into a large rectangle. Draw calculator buttons with a bright colored marker. (It helps to have a calculator on hand to go by to get it right). Paint or color the calculator black and the buttons a bright color.

Sundial

Begin with a modern birdbath.

Cut a large triangle out of cardboard and cover with aluminum foil or paint it gold.

Have someone hold completed triangle upright in birdbath while it is filled with stones. The stones will brace it upright.

Tip: You can use play dough to attach it to the bottom for greater stability.

Swords for Soldiers

Draw the outline of a sword on cardboard. Cut the shape out (as one piece).

Wrap the "blade" portion with aluminum foil and wrap the "handle" with black electrical tape.

Throne

Drape a chair with arms in a very rich fabric such as velvet. Chenille throws could be substituted. On each arm, tie a large, long tassel (such as can be found in drapery stores). Tie two of these to the back of the "throne" for further opulence.

If you use a chair without arms, just use the tassels on the back of the chair.

Scenery

For Jesus and Disciples (also any others "listening to Jesus"):

"Parables of the Lost": Set to one side of the stage a low table and floor pillows to sit on OR a long table of regular height and chairs.

All other parable dramas: A "rock" for Jesus to sit on. (All those "listening to Jesus" will be seated on the "ground.")

For the rock, you may actually use a large boulder or use a child-sized chair covered with a painter's drop cloth or dark fabric.

Market Place

To create a marketplace that can quickly be set up just use people carrying jars and baskets with their "wares." (Might have some signs hung in the area.)

Or use card tables and TV trays draped with sheets or large tablecloths as "market booths." Signs can be attached to the front of each "booth." Card tables already covered and with a sign can each be carried in and out by two people. TV trays already draped can be carried by one person.

Mr. Bigg's Tent for Parable of the Talents

To create the feel of being in a "large opulent tent" (Mr. Bigg's place of business) you may wish to paint it as a backdrop.

If you are going to be performing in the sanctuary, gym, or other open space, you will need a "portable" tent. It can just be implied, or you may drape fabrics over chalkboards on wheels or portable room dividers.

Pigsty

To create a "pigsty" for "Parables of the Lost" simply toss a rumpled dark brown or black piece of cloth or blanket on the floor.

If you wish to make further scenery, set a "fence" in front of the cloth or blanket. A strip of fence can be made from simple boards and nailed to a wooden base.

To use this option you will need the help and/or supervision of a carpenter.

Door

Doors may simply be implied by a person standing at one side of the stage. This can be enhanced by hanging a sign (such as the "INN" sign for "The Good Samaritan") over the place where the door would be.

If you would like a doorway, one can be fashioned (with the help of a carpenter) out of simple wood. (No need for a real door.)

Or use a large refrigerator box and, on the front, cut the top, bottom, and one side so that it will open. Paint it to look like a door with a knob.

Vineyard

The vineyard will be implied, but to enhance the effect you can make part of the vineyard.

Drape dried grapevine wreaths over sawhorses and tie on some artificial grapes. Or make bunches of grapes by drawing them on posterboard and painting them. Cut out the grape clusters you have made and glue them to the grapevine.

Dramas

Abingdon Press hereby grants permission to original purchaser to reproduce the material contained on pages 53-96 of this publication for purpose of rehearsal and performance, provided the following notice appears on each copy:

Copyright © 2009 by Abingdon Press. All rights reserved.

PRODUCTION NOTE FOR ALL DRAMAS:

Where multiple characters are to be speaking at the same time, as in this example—

> **Disciples:** Oooh! Oooh! / Call on me, Jesus. / I got this one. / Yeah, I understand this parable. / I know who the neighbor is. / Yeah. Even if he's supposed to be an enemy. / Tricky, huh?

—break it down and assign the different parts. Tweens are not good at doing this without assignments.

Parables of the Lost

Based on Luke 15:1-32

Production Notes

Combine roles for small groups. As with all the dramas, the actors in the parables come from the group seated around Jesus and can possibly return there instead of exiting. However, the Pharisees and Scribes do NOT come from this group, although Scribe One will join the group at the end.

Open on Jesus sitting at a table, upstage, eating with disciples and others. (Table can stay on stage the whole time and be used for the welcoming-home party, as long as there is room downstage for acting out parables.) Actors get up from table to act out parables.

Speaking Roles
Pharisee One
Pharisee Two
Scribe One
Scribe Two
Jesus
Shepherd
Woman
Father (a wealthy farmer)
Older Son
Younger Son
Merchant(s)
Gambler
Wine Merchant
Pig Farmer
Pig
Servant One
Servant Two
Servant Three

Nonspeaking Roles: Optional
pigs
any number of disciples
any number of Pharisees
any number of people in the market

Props

table (if using low table, everyone can sit on the floor; if taller table, chairs will be needed); baskets, bottles or jars, and/or signs for merchants to carry; tables for marketplace; pair of dice for gambler; coin pouch and coins for younger son; rake or hoe for older son

Two Pharisees and two scribes enter and look at Jesus and people gathered at table.

Pharisee One: What is going on here?

Pharisee Two: Disgusting!

Scribe One: This man, Jesus, teaches about goodness and then eats with sinners and tax collectors.

Scribe Two: Should I write that down?

Jesus rises in order to speak to the Pharisees and scribes face to face. Someone gets up from the table to play the shepherd.

Jesus: *(to Pharisees and scribes)* Which one of you, having a hundred sheep and losing one of them, does not leave the ninety-nine in the wilderness and go after the one that is lost?

Shepherd: I'll be right back. You be good.

People at the table "Baaaa!" in response. Shepherd looks around, maybe into the audience. He goes to edge of stage, miming finding a sheep and putting it on his back.

Jesus: When he has found it, he lays it on his shoulders and rejoices. . . . He calls together his friends and neighbors, saying to them,

Shepherd: Rejoice with me, for I have found my sheep that was lost.

Pharisee One: What does some shepherd have to do with your eating with tax collectors and sinners?

Jesus: I tell you, there will be more joy in heaven over one sinner who repents than over ninety-nine righteous persons who need no repentance.

Lights come up on the table of people. The Pharisees and scribes look upon Jesus and his companions, shaking their heads in disgust.

Pharisee One: So, you're saying that God loves them more than us?

Jesus: What woman having ten silver coins, if she loses one of them, does not search carefully until she finds it?

Woman: *(getting up from the table, looking around)* Excuse me. Excuse me. Where did I put that coin?

Woman looks around the Pharisees.

Woman: Excuse me. Excuse me. I must find my coin.

Woman lifts up the foot of either scribe and sees the coin.

Woman: Ah ha! There it is. He was standing on it the whole time!

Scribe Two: Should I write that down?

Jesus: When she has found it, she calls together her friends and neighbors, saying,

Woman: Rejoice with me, for I have found the coin that I had lost.

Pharisee Two: Sheep and coins. Coins and sheep. Can't you talk straight? Why should we believe what you preach when you spend so much time with such people?

Jesus: Okay. Let's talk people. *(pause)* There was a man who had two sons . . .

Lights go down. Jesus, Pharisees, and scribes move off to side of stage. Jesus mimes talking to Pharisees and scribes until lights come up.

Vignette One: Father's Farm

Lights come up on the father and two sons upstage.

Father: You two are good boys.

Older Son: Well, there's work to be done in some of the fields. I'll see you later, Papa.

Younger Son: You know, Pop, I gotta tell ya, I'm just not cut out to be a farmer. The big city, that's for me.

Father: Well, son, you have many talents, but you're right. You're not a farmer.

Younger Son: So, Pop, could you give me my share of the farm and everything now?

Father: It makes me very sad to hear you say that, son. But I suppose you need to experience the city life for yourself. I'll give you your share now.

Vignette Two: City Market

Jesus: A few days later, the younger son gathered all he had and "hit the road," journeying to a distant land.

The younger son goes into the audience, walks around, muttering things like "Oh boy" and "I can't wait" and "Babylon or Bust." Meanwhile, stage fills with people as in a market: merchants calling out, a drunk person weaving or passed out, a thief picking pockets, a gambler throwing dice.

The younger son enters the marketplace.

Merchant: Hey you! You want to buy some almonds?

Younger Son: Sure. *(pulling out several coins)* I'm not very good at the exchange rate, though.

Merchant: *(grabbing all the coins out of his hand)* Yeah. That's just enough.

Younger Son: Boy, almonds are expensive around here.

Gambler: Hey you! You want to play some dice?

Younger Son: I don't know. It looks like fun.

Gambler: Sure, it's loads of fun. Everyone's a winner.

Younger Son: Well, then. If everyone's a winner . . . *(throws dice)*

Gambler: Oh, sorry. You lose.

Younger Son: Hey. I thought you said everyone's a winner.

Gambler: My mistake. *(takes money and moves away)*

Wine Merchant: Cheer up. Have some wine. You'll feel better.

Younger Son: I don't know. The wine's not as much as the almonds, is it?

Wine Merchant: Well, after a few sips, you won't care as much.

Younger Son: That sounds good. I'll take a bottle.

Wine Merchant: *(grabs a lot of money)* Bon appétit.

Younger Son: Hey! It was as much as the almonds! *(takes a big gulp)* But, you're right. I don't care.

Younger son dances around crazily, giving coins to merchants.

Vignette Three: Pig Farm

Younger Son: *(emerging, dazed, from behind the curtain)* Wow! That was almost as expensive as almonds too. *(reaches into coin pouch)* Speaking of which . . . *(pulls out empty hand)* Wow! I'm broke. I've squandered all my inheritance on reck-HIC on reck-HIC on reck-HIC . . . on wild living.

Pig Farmer: *(pigs squeal)* I hear you need a job.

Younger Son: I guess so. I'm pretty experienced at farming. I had a farm before I spent everything on wine, women, and almonds.

Pig Farmer: Okay. I guess I'll let you take care of these pigs.

Younger Son: Gee thanks, mister. I'll take good care of 'em. You'll see. *(gets down on all fours to play with them)* Hey, piggie, piggie.

Jesus: After a while, the younger son got tired of seeing the pigs get fat while he was starving.

Younger Son: You said it. I'd eat the corncobs but the farmer wants them all for his pigs. (*A pig comes up and pushes him out of the way and eats something he was sitting on.*) And the pigs want them all for the pigs too.

Pig: You know something? All your complaining is making us all nervous. If you're so unhappy, why don't you just go back home and say to your father, "Look, father. I've sinned against heaven and you. I am certainly not worthy to be called your son. But, if you'll hire me back as a servant, I'll work really hard." Then, at least you won't starve to death.

Younger Son: *(stares at pig)* I had no idea pigs are so smart.

Pig: We are smart. But you are just hallucinating from hunger and thirst.

Vignette Four: Father's Farm

Younger Son: Whatever. You're absolutely right. It's been great rolling around with you, but this son is going home!

Pig: Yee-haw. Now maybe the sows will calm down and I'll get some sleep.

The younger son exits. The father and the older son stand as at the beginning.

Older Son: Well, Papa. There's work to be done in the fields. At least the ones we still have left.

Father: You're a good son.

Older Son: Right. Well, I'll see you at supper time. *(heads off into audience with his farm implement)*

Father: You're a good farmer too.

The younger son comes from behind audience, different part than where the older son is. The father does a double-take, seeing the younger son.

Father: *(staring in disbelief)* Son? My younger son? *(realizes it is him and runs to greet him out in the audience)* My son! My son!

Father hugs younger son.

Father: You're alive! You're alive! I can't believe it. I can hardly believe my hands, not to mention my eyes. *(hugs him again)*

Younger Son: I have something to say, Pop. I know I've sinned against heaven and against you. I am not worthy to be your son.

Father: *(walking back toward stage with younger son)* Let's see, now. We'll have to have a feast to celebrate. I'll send someone to invite all the neighbors and relatives. And someone needs to gather some corn and vegetables. And I'll tell the cooks . . . *(yelling to servants)* Ho, there. You!

Servant One: Yes, sir?

Father: Bring my best robe. This is my son!

Servant One: Yes, sir.

Father: And you. Get him a ring. And some shoes.

Servant Two: Yes, sir.

Father: You. Tell the hands and the cooks to kill and cook the fatted calf.

Servant Three: Yes, sir.

The servants exit. If, during the parable, the actors have left the table, they should return so that it's full of people again.

Father: *(now center stage, makes a toast, looking at the guests and the audience)* Everyone. To my younger son! He was dead and now is alive. He was lost and is now found.

All: Hear! Hear!

Music starts. There is great celebrating and adlibbing of lines like "Pass the sauce" and "Mmm. This is great." And "Where did you go?" The younger son sits at the table. Father stands looking out at the audience.

Father: I'll be right back. *(going out to his older son)*

Older Son: Hello, Papa. I still have quite a bit of work to do if we will ever make harvest.

Father: Son! Your brother has come home. Please, come into the house. Let's all feast together.

Older Son: I can't, Papa. I have served you all these years without complaining. I've never, ever disobeyed you. But, did you ever give me a young goat to celebrate with my friends? No, you didn't. But this son of yours, who wasted away half your property on who knows what, you kill the fatted calf for him?

Father: *(trying to hug him even though the older son is pulling away)* My son. My son. You are always with me. And all that is mine is yours. But come, celebrate. Your own brother. He was dead. He was lost. Now he's found. He's alive.

Older Son: I still have some work to do. Then I need to put away the tools. Then feed the animals.

Father: The servants can do that.

Older Son: I want to do it. Then I need to wash up.

Father: Then I'll see you in there in a bit?

Older Son: In a while. Perhaps.

Father: You must come, son. *(walks back to the stage)*

Older Son: I know, Papa. I know.

All actors sit at table, except Pharisees, scribes, and Jesus. These come center stage.

Pharisee One: So, did the older son join the feast?

Jesus: Will you join us?

Pharisee Two: We have to get back. We have some . . . uh . . . an appointment.

Scribe One: *(meekly)* I would like to join you. If you will have me.

Jesus: Certainly. All are welcome. *(to the Pharisees and the other scribe)* I guess you have your answer.

Scribe Two: *(to the Pharisees)* Should I write that down?

Jesus and Scribe One sit at the table. The Pharisees and Scribe Two exit.

Scribe One: Could you pass some of that fatted calf, please?

All laugh.

The Unforgiving Servant

Based on Matthew 18:23-35

Production Notes

Combine roles for small groups. Four disciples with speaking parts could easily double with nonspeaking roles or could take servant roles in the parable.

Disciples (and if a large group, others) are gathered around Jesus, who is seated on a "rock" or something so that they all can see him. Those who act out the parable could come from this gathering, putting on a robe or helmet or crown to get into the role, or they could enter from backstage.

Speaking Roles
Peter
Andrew
Jesus
John
Bartholomew
King
Accountant
Servant One
Servant Two
Unforgiving Servant
Poor Servant

Nonspeaking Roles
King's servants *(bring in throne—could be same actors as Servant One and Servant Two)*
two guards (soldiers)
any number of disciples

Props

chair with arms (throne), table, chair, calculator for the accountant, coins for servants

Optional: swords for guards

Peter: Lord, I have a question. Andrew and I were discussing forgiveness, and we were wondering how many times we should forgive someone who wrongs us. Is seven times enough?

Jesus: Not seven times, but, I tell you, seventy-seven times.

Andrew: That's a lot, Lord.

Jesus: For this reason the kingdom of heaven can be compared to a king who wished to settle accounts with his servants.

King enters, followed by guards and two servants who bring his throne. He sits. His accountant enters, either standing or sitting at a desk with a calculator. Other servants enter, lining up to pay at the accountant's table.

John: Oh boy. A parable. I love parables.

Bartholomew: Me too. At least, the ones I can understand.

Accountant: Let's see. One pig, three talents. Two big jars, fifty cents. A piece of cloth, eleven cents. That'll be three-sixty-one.

Servant One: Whew! Here you go. *(exits or sits down at table)*

Accountant: *(to next servant)* Five pigeons. That's two-thirty-two.

Servant Two: Great. Keep the change.

The unforgiving servant enters, trembling.

Accountant: Boy, oh boy. *(reading from a long list)* Thirty-two pigs, eighteen late charges, fifty pigeons, ten jars of myrrh, three hundred bottles of wine, two donkeys, etc., etc., etc., etc. That'll be ten thousand talents.

Unforgiving Servant: Uh, that much? Are you sure?

Accountant: Don't make me total it up again. It will probably come out even more.

Unforgiving Servant. Uh, right, okay. So, how much do you want today?

Accountant: All of it.

King: What's the problem here? Can't you pay what you owe?

Unforgiving Servant: Certainly, sire. Well, some of it, anyway.

King: How much?

Unforgiving Servant: Uh. How about a buck fifty?

King: What? That's an outrage. How dare you? Guards! Take this man away and sell him into slavery. Take his family, too, and sell them. And sell all his possessions.

Unforgiving Servant: *(bowing down on the ground)* Oh, please, sire. Please! I'm just going through a rough patch. Please don't sell me or my family. I'll repay you. My kids have been sick, and my mother-in-law eats more than three horses, and my father, who was helping me, broke his leg, and I promise I'll pay. Just don't sell my family into slavery. Please. Have mercy!

King: Alright. Alright. I know what mothers-in-law are like. I have ten of them. I forgive you all your debts.

Unforgiving Servant: Oh, thank you, your majesty. You are truly the greatest king in the whole world. Thank you. Thank you.

King: Just get back to work, so you don't owe any more.

Unforgiving Servant: Yes, sir. Right away, sire. *(exits)*

Accountant: Next!

King and courtiers exit. The accountant is gathering up his papers and such, maybe counting the money, and stays onstage.

Jesus: But that same servant, as he went out, came upon one of his fellow servants who owed him a hundred denarii.

The unforgiving servant enters. The poor servant enters and comes up to him. The accountant watches the whole thing.

Poor Servant: Hey, Ralph. How ya doin'? Look, I know I owe you those denarii for those baskets of figs. I can't pay you today, but I—

Unforgiving Servant: *(grabs him)* What?!! You can't pay me? What do you mean you can't pay me?

Poor Servant: *(choking)* I . . . mean . . . I can't . . . pay . . . *today* . . . but . . . I will pay. You're choking me.

Unforgiving Servant: *(letting go)* Pay me right this minute, or else.

Poor Servant: I can't. Please. You know I'll pay you back. My donkey hurt his leg, my boy is sick, and my mother-in-law—

Unforgiving Servant: Don't tell me about your mother-in-law. If you can't pay me, I'm having you put in prison until you pay. *(calling out)* Guards! Guards!

Two guards enter and take hold of the arms of the poor servant.

Unforgiving Servant: Take this man away. Throw him in jail until he pays me what he owes me.

Poor Servant: Please! Can't you show a little forgiveness? A few days are all I ask. Please!

Unforgiving Servant: What are you waiting for? Take him away.

Poor Servant: Please. Show a little mercy. Just a little kindness! Please!

The guards take him away. The unforgiving servant turns around and sees the accountant staring at him in disbelief.

Unforgiving Servant: What are you looking at? *(exits)*

King, servants, guards, and courtiers enter. King sits on throne. Accountant sits back at table.

Jesus: When the king learned about what the man had done, he sent for him.

King: Bring me that guy with the mother-in-law.

The unforgiving servant enters. A couple of guards move close.

King: Refresh my memory, you wicked little man. Didn't you come in here just a few hours ago, owing *me* ten thousand talents!

Unforgiving Servant: Uh, yes, your majesty.

King: And didn't you drop to the floor and plead for mercy?

Unforgiving Servant: Uh, yes, your majesty.

King: And didn't I show you mercy and forgive you this enormous debt?

Unforgiving Servant: Uh, yes, your majesty.

King: And didn't you just run into a man who owes you a teeny-weeny, tiny, itty-bitty, little, so small, insignificant, practically nothing bit of money, for a couple of baskets of figs?

Unforgiving Servant: But, sire . . .

King: Answer my question!

Unforgiving Servant: Uh, yes, your majesty.

King: And not only did you not forgive him, but you actually had him thrown into jail!? For figs!?

Unforgiving Servant: Well, you see, sire . . . uh, yes, your majesty.

King: So, rather than follow my example of kindness, forgiveness, and mercy, you do exactly the opposite of what your king does for you. So, all I can imagine is that you must think that you are somehow better, more important, smarter, etc., etc., than your king. For why else would you not do the same thing for someone else that I did for you?

Unforgiving Servant: Uh, because I needed the money?

King: Guards. Take him away. Put him in the cell that used to hold the man who owed him money.

Unforgiving Servant: Wrong answer? *(as he's being taken away)*

Accountant: Wrong answer.

Unforgiving Servant: I don't suppose it would help if I groveled again, would it?

Peter: *(jumping up, excited)* I get it. I get this parable! The king is like . . . God, right?

Andrew: And the servants, they're us! I mean, not the unforgiving one, of course, but the ones who . . . uh . . . owe each other?

Jesus: You must forgive your brother or your sister from your heart if you expect your heavenly Father to forgive you.

Peter: Got it!

Andrew: Seventy-seven times. No problem.

Peter: Lord, what kind of jail would God throw us into anyway?

Andrew: Uh, Peter, let's not go there.

Peter: Got it. Never mind, Lord. Never mind.

The Good Samaritan

Based on Luke 10:25-37

Production Notes

Combine roles for small groups.

Open on Jesus sitting on a rock, teaching a group of disciples and others. As with all of the dramas, the players in the parable would come from the group and can possibly return there instead of exiting. When "Various Disciples" are to speak, divide up what is to be said. They are to be making comments to one another, many at the same time.

Speaking Roles
Lawyer
Jesus
Man
Robber One
Robber Two
Robber Three
Priest
Levite
Samaritan
Innkeeper
Various Disciples (only
   as part of group)

Nonspeaking Roles
Optional: "donkey"
possibly crowd members
   around Jesus

Props
travel pouches (or backpack or duffel bag) for man

Optional: clubs for robbers,
donkey for good Samaritan, sign saying "Inn"

Vignette One: Roadside

Lawyer: *(raises his hand or stands up)* Teacher, I have a question.

Jesus: Yes?

Lawyer: *(speaking aggressively)* Teacher, I want to know what I need to do to inherit this eternal life you speak about.

Jesus: What is written in the law? What do you read there?

Lawyer: It's very clear. It says to love the Lord your God with all your heart and with all your soul, with all your strength and with all your mind. And it says to love your neighbor as yourself.

Jesus: You have given the right answer; do this, and you will live.

Lawyer: And who is my neighbor?

Jesus looks at the lawyer in disbelief. The others look around at him. He meekly sits down.

Jesus: A man was going down from Jerusalem to Jericho . . .

Man enters from group.

Man: Oh, boy. I love Jericho. I can't wait.

Jesus: . . . and fell suddenly into the hands of robbers.

Three robbers jump out at the man.

Robber One: What's the matter, dude? Don't you know you shouldn't travel this road alone?

Robber Two: I think as a reminder you should give us your boots.

Robber Three: Oh, he needs a better reminder than that. I think we need to take his cloak and bags and, yes, his money.

They take all of his stuff.

Robber One: You know, with this fellow, I think he needs a better reminder even than that.

Man: No, no. Thanks, though. I'll remember. Really!

Robber One: You say that. Then, next year, you'll be back on this road alone. Or some other road. Who knows?

Man: No. Strictly carpools from now on.

Robber Two: I think we better make *(pretends to hit him in the stomach)* **really sure!**

Robber One: *("hitting" him too)* Yeah! Positive!

Robber Three: Hey! Why do I have to be the one to hold the stuff while you guys get to beat our victims senseless? It's not fair.

Jesus: The robbers stripped him, beat him, and went away, leaving him half dead. Now by chance a priest was going down that road.

Priest enters. He walks close by the man and sees him and hears him groaning.

Priest: Mercy! Are you dead?

Man groans and cries out for help.

Priest: I guess you're not dead, but you're awfully bloody. I'm sorry, but I just don't have time to help you. I have to be in the next town soon. Besides, I can't get blood on my hands or I will be officially unclean, and I have religious duties to perform! Sorry!

The priest walks to the other side of the road and into the audience.

Priest: *(to audience member)* Friend, even if you're not a priest, watch out for that bloody almost-dead man up there. You don't want to get blood on your hands either.

The priest exits.

Jesus: So likewise a Levite came to the place and saw him.

Levite: Goodness! What a mess that man is in. *(looking around)* I better not help him. It may be a trap. *(moving away from him)* I think it's safer on this side of the road. If I see someone down the road, maybe I'll send him back to help the man.

The Levite continues down into the audience.

Levite: *(to a different audience member)* Watch out if you're going that way. There's a man who is badly hurt on the side of the road. You'd better stay on that side *(points to the side away from the man)* . . . in case it's a trap.

The Levite exits.

Jesus: But a Samaritan while traveling came near him.

Samaritan enters with donkey.

Various Disciples: Boo! / Hiss! / You know a Samaritan would never help anyone. / Not even another Samaritan. / Yeah. They're lazy. / Yes. Mean too. / Yeah. He's not going to help.

Man groans and cries out for help.

Samaritan: Who is that? Where is that sound coming from?

Man: *(groaning, breathing heavily)* Over here. I've been robbed. Beaten. Left for dead.

Samaritan: Oh, you poor man. Here, let me help you. *(running back to donkey)*

Man: Oh, please. You're not going to leave too?!

Samaritan: No, I'm just getting some bandages. *(gets some supplies and runs back to man)* See? Before I move you, I need to bandage some of your wounds.

Man: I'm sorry I'm bloody. Please, don't leave.

Samaritan: I'm not leaving. Here, this ointment will sting at first, but it will help.

Man: Ow! Oooh!

Samaritan: It's okay. It's not too deep. Here. The bandages will work. Let me help you up.

The Samaritan helps the man, groaning, to stand, but the man falters.

Samaritan: That's okay. Don't put any more weight on that leg. You're in no shape to walk. You'll ride on my donkey. Here let me help you. It's going to hurt, but then you'll be okay.

The Samaritan helps the man onto the donkey. They walk slowly, or in place, center stage.

Man: Thank you. You're the kindest man I've ever met.

Samaritan: You would have done the same for me.

Man: You're a Samaritan, aren't you?

Samaritan: Yes.

Man: But still you helped me. My name is Joseph.

Samaritan: Call me Benjamin.

Man: You are such a good man, Benjamin.

Samaritan: You should probably save your energy . . . Joseph. Get some sleep.

Lights dim.

Vignette Two: Inn

Lights come up. Man and Samaritan walk to one side of stage. Man slumps on floor. The Samaritan knocks. Innkeeper opens the door.

Innkeeper: No donkeys allowed. You'll have to take it around back.

Samaritan: Friend, I need a room for this man. And I'll need some fresh bandages and ointment.

Innkeeper: *(looks again)* Oh. I didn't even see him.

Samaritan: He's very badly hurt. He was robbed and beaten. Help me get him to a room.

Innkeeper: But if he was robbed, he won't be able to pay.

Samaritan: I will pay you, sir. Now, please help me.

Samaritan and innkeeper lift the man and carry him inside. The two then come back outside. The Samaritan reaches for the pouches on the donkey.

Samaritan: I have to leave early in the morning. But here is some money. You will take care of him. If you have any extra expenses, I will pay you on my way back. Is that alright with you?

Innkeeper: Sure. Sure. *(pause)* Just one thing, though. How do I know you will actually stop back by here?

Samaritan: I've given my word. Are you doubting it?

Innkeeper: Well, uh . . . if you give your word, that's good enough for me.

Samaritan: Thank you, sir!

The Samaritan takes the donkey and exits. The innkeeper goes back inside.

The lawyer, still in the group, stands up, where he was at the beginning of the parable.

Jesus: *(to the lawyer)* Which of these three, do you think, was a neighbor to the man who fell into the hands of the robber?

Disciples: Oooh! Oooh! / Call on me, Jesus. / I got this one. / Yeah, I understand this parable. / I know who the neighbor is. / Yeah. Even if he's supposed to be an enemy. / Tricky, huh?

Lawyer: The Samaritan is the neighbor, I suppose. Because he shows mercy, and he helps him.

Jesus: Go and do likewise.

Parable of the Talents

Based on Matthew 25:14-30

Production Notes

Combine roles for small groups.

Open on Jesus sitting on a rock, teaching a group of disciples and others. As with all of the dramas, the players in the parable would come from the group, and can possibly return there instead of exiting. This is a combination biblical and modernized version of the parable. This is done to make it more understandable.

Speaking Roles
Jesus
Disciples
Assistant
Mr. Bigg
Mary
Isaac
Jonah

Nonspeaking Roles
any number of disciples

Props

"papers" for everyone, a watch for Mr. Bigg (you may want to make an oversized watch for him or a clock for the "wall"), chairs

Jesus: God wants you to be like lights shining in all that you do.

Disciples: *(puzzled)* Lights shining? / Lord, what does that mean? / I'm sorry, Lord. I don't understand. / You want us to be brighter?

Jesus: You reflect God's glory in all the good things you do for others with your God-given talents. Not using those talents is like hiding your light when others need it.

Disciples: Oh, I get it. / I think I get it. / I see. / God wants us to use our abilities to help others? / Right?

Jesus: A man, going on a journey, summoned his slaves and entrusted his property to them.

Vignette One: Businessman's Office

Enter Mr. Bigg (the businessman), standing and reading some papers. Assistant enters with his chair. Mr. Bigg sits down.

Assistant: The servants you requested are here, Mr. Bigg. Should I send them in?

Bigg: *(reading)* Yes. Thank you, William. *(looks up)* Actually, send them in one at a time, please.

Assistant: Yes, sir.

Assistant exits. First servant, Mary, enters. They shake hands.

Mary: You sent for me, Mister Bigg?

Bigg: Yes . . . uh . . .

Mary: Oh, Mary, sir.

Bigg: Yes, Mary. I am going on a trip, and I would like to test you out.

Mary: Test me out, sir?

Bigg: Yes. I'm going to leave you in charge of fifty thousand dollars to take care of however you see fit. I'll be back in a month and you'll report then how much you've made.

Mary: Great. Thank you, Mr. Bigg. I won't let you down.

Both stand up and shake hands. Mary exits. Assistant enters.

Assistant: Would you like to see Isaac now, sir?

Bigg: Yes. Thank you. Send him in, please.

Assistant exits. Isaac enters. They shake hands.

Isaac: Hello, Mr. Bigg, it's a pleasure to see you.

Bigg: Have a seat, Isaac. As I told Mary, I'm going on a trip and I wonder if you're up for a little test I have in mind.

Isaac: Yes, sir. Whatever it is, sir. I am ready.

Bigg: Great. I'm going to leave you in charge of twenty-five thousand dollars to take care of however you see fit. I'll be back in a month and you'll report then how much you've made.

Isaac: Great. Thank you, sir. I won't let you down.

Both stand up and shake hands. Isaac leaves. Assistant enters.

Assistant: The last servant is here, sir. Jonah.

Bigg: You mean to say he was late?

Assistant: A little bit, yes sir.

Bigg: A little?

Assistant: Well, actually, sir, he was a half hour late. He got lost and wound up in the mail room.

Bigg: The mail room? Can't he read directions? Is he crazy?

Assistant: It's not for me to say so, sir.

Bigg: *(wearily)* Alright. Send him in, I suppose.

Assistant: Yes, sir.

Assistant exits. No one enters. Bigg waits and watches. Nobody enters. Bigg stands and approaches the door. Jonah pops his head in warily.

Jonah: Are you ready to see me, sir?

Assistant: Yes, of course. Didn't my assistant tell you to come in?

Jonah: Well, yes, but I just wanted to make sure.

Bigg: Come in, Jonah. Have a seat.

Bigg extends his hand. Jonah doesn't see it before he sits down. He catches himself, stands back up and extends his hand just as Bigg retracts his hand and sits down. Bigg stands back up as Jonah retracts his hand and sits. Finally, Bigg (rolling his eyes) and Jonah manage to stand at same time and shake hands. Both sit.

Bigg: The reason I've called you here, Jonah, is that I am going on a trip and I'd like to give a few of my servants a little test.

Jonah: A test? As in a real live test?

Bigg: Yes. That's what I said.

Jonah: Here's the thing, Mr. Bigg. . . . I'm . . . uh . . . not really very good at tests. There was this one time in the third grade, I actually threw up . . .

Jonah sees that Bigg is getting angry.

Jonah: But, if you like, I guess I could take this test. I probably won't throw up.

Bigg: I'm going to put you in charge of five thousand dollars, Jonah. When I get back in a month I want to hear what you've done with the money.

Jonah: Five thousand dollars, Mr. Bigg? Are you sure?

Bigg: I don't think you want to hear the answer to that, Jonah. Now get busy. I want a full report in a month.

Jonah: Thanks, Mr. Bigg. I'll try not to disappoint you.

They shake hands. Jonah exits. Assistant enters.

Assistant: The caravan is waiting, Mr. Bigg. I've booked you in business class. A two-hump camel with lots of padding, confirmed. Your bags are already on it. Bon voyage, as they say.

Bigg: Thank you, William. I appreciate how organized you always are. I know that I can count on you. That means a lot to me.

Assistant: Thank you, Mr. Bigg. Have a great time.

Bigg and the assistant exit.

Vignette Two: Businessman's Office

Mary, Isaac, and Jonah enter. Each has a group around him/her. The people in the groups can return to Jesus' group instead of exiting.

Mary: *(to different people around her, who take off with their orders)* I want half that in olive oil, a quarter in the cedars of Lebanon, and buy that olive press on the east side of town too.

Isaac: *(to different people around him, who take off with their orders)* We're going to corner the market on goat cheese. Also, I want you to double production on the extra-large clay jars. That's right. Extra-large only!

Jonah: *(to different people around him)* Uh, can I get back to you on that? I'll think that over. Yes, I promise I'll get back to you too.

The people surrounding Jonah throw up their hands in disgust and exit shaking their heads. Assistant enters, carrying papers. He gives some to Mary.

Assistant: These are the reports for this week, Mary.

Mary: Thank you, William. Could you let the silversmiths know I'd like to speak with them, please?

Assistant: Will do.

Mary: Thank you.

Assistant gives some papers to Isaac.

Assistant: The reports for this week, Isaac.

Isaac: Thank you, William. Do you mind telling those horse traders I'll be with them soon? And confirm the appointment with the silk traders.

Assistant: Will do.

Isaac: Thank you.

Assistant gives one piece of paper to Jonah.

Assistant: The take-out menu you asked for, Jonah.

Jonah: Oh, good. I'm hungry.

Assistant: Is that all you need, Jonah?

Jonah: I guess so. Thanks. Oh. You can cancel my massage this afternoon. And send word to my mother that I'll be home for dinner.

Assistant: Right.

Assistant exits. Then Mary, Isaac, and Jonah exit.

Vignette Three: Businessman's Office

Bigg enters, reading some papers.

Jesus: After a long time the master came to settle accounts with them.

Assistant enters with chair. Bigg sits.

Assistant: Welcome back, sir. I hope you had a pleasant trip.

Bigg: I tell you, William, if I don't see another camel as long as I live, it will be too soon.

Assistant: Should I send in Mary?

Bigg: Send in all three, please.

Assistant: Yes, sir.

Assistant exits. Mary, Isaac, and Jonah enter.

Bigg: I'm a little tired, folks. But I wanted to hear how you did with the money I entrusted to you.

Mary: So far, sir, my group has made another fifty thousand dollars, doubling your investment.

Bigg: Excellent, Mary. Good work!

Mary: Thank you, Mr. Bigg.

Isaac: My group has made twenty-five thousand dollars, sir. And counting!

Bigg: Excellent, Isaac. You doubled your investment too! Good work. And Jonah?

Jonah: Yes, sir! Five thousand dollars. It's all there!

Bigg: Excellent. All three of you doubled your money.

Jonah: Doubled? No, I mean the five thousand dollars that you gave me, I still have it. I didn't lose it. It's safe and sound.

Bigg: You mean to say that you didn't make a dime?

Jonah: Well, uh, I heard you were a tough customer, so I wanted to make sure my plan was rock solid before I put it into motion. And I'm almost ready to start the first phase of it.

Bigg: Meanwhile, where is the money?

Jonah: *(whispering to Bigg)* It's buried in my Mom's backyard!

Bigg: Jonah, did it occur to you that if you had only opened a child's passbook savings account, you would have made at least a few dollars? You think I'm a tough customer? I'll show you a tough customer. I want you to get a shovel, go home, dig up the money, bring it back here, and give it to Mary.

Jonah: But she already has fifty thousand.

Bigg: Actually, she now has one hundred thousand. Correction. One hundred five thousand, counting yours.

Jonah: So, I failed the test.

Bigg: Gee, you think?

Jonah: Well, at least I didn't throw up. So, what do you want me to do?

Bigg: I believe you have some digging to do.

Jonah: Right. Uh, I better be going. *(starts to leave)*

Bigg: Get that money to Mary before your lunch hour is over, Jonah.

Jonah: Right. Right away. *(starts to exit, then stops)* Does that mean I have to skip lunch?

Bigg: Get out of here! *(Jonah exits.)*

The other characters exit or go back to the group as Jesus is speaking.

Jesus: So, if I tell you to go out and make use of your talents, what do you think that means?

Disciples: Invest wisely? / To get rich, right? / Buy low, sell high?

Jesus: Do you think I'm talking about investing money? Or do you think I'm talking about investing yourselves and your talents?

Disciples: Darn. / Oh well. / Something told me we weren't in one of those get-rich-quick seminars.

Jesus: Does God want you to get rich yourselves, like the tax collectors? Or does God want you to use your talents to enrich the lives of your friends and your neighbors? Which one is really letting your light shine?

Disciples: *(all)* Enriching the lives of others.

Jesus: That is what the kingdom of God is all about. And, truly, there are no greater riches than that.

Disciples: Really? / Come on! / Is that true? / Really?

Jesus: Count on it.

Laborers in the Vineyard

Based on Matthew 20:1–16

Production Notes

Open on Jesus sitting on a rock, teaching a group of disciples and others. As with all of the dramas, the players in the parable would come from the group and can possibly return there instead of exiting.

Market place is center stage. The vineyard where "grapes are picked" is actually in the aisles of the audience. If an actor is doubling in another role instead of "picking grapes," the actor exits behind the audience and returns to the stage.

Speaking Roles
John
Other Disciples
Jesus
Vineyard Owner
Worker One
Worker Two
Worker Three
Worker Four
Worker Five
Worker Six
Worker Seven
Workers Eight
Worker Nine
Worker Ten
Worker Eleven
Assistant

Nonspeaking Roles
Optional: "donkey"
possibly crowd members
    around Jesus

Props
coins for paying laborers, watch or sundial for vineyard owner, baskets for workers

John: Jesus, we were discussing the kingdom of heaven and we don't quite get it. Could you explain it for us please?

Other Disciples: Yes! / Yeah. / I don't get it at all. / Please, Jesus. / Right. How do you get into it? / Where is it? / Is it coming?

Jesus: The kingdom of heaven is like a landowner who went out early in the morning to hire laborers for his vineyard.

Vineyard Owner: Well, it looks like it's harvest time. I better go find some workers to pick my grapes.

Disciples around Jesus raise their hands and call out, as if in school.

Disciples: Oooh! Oooh! / Me. Me. / Please pick me. / Come on. I can pick grapes.

Owner: Okay. You. You. And you!

Three stand up, excited.

A Disciple: I never get picked.

Owner: It's almost dawn. If you guys work till sunset picking my grapes, I'll give you each a denarius.

Worker One: Wow! You're kidding!

Worker Two: Man, you're a generous boss.

Worker Three: Yeah, we'll work for you anytime.

They head out into the audience to "pick grapes."

Jesus: When he went out about nine o'clock, he saw others standing idle in the marketplace *(three around Jesus jump up)*, and he said to them,

Owner: If you guys work in my fields picking grapes till sunset, I'll give you a fair wage.

Worker Four: Well, you seem like an honest fellow.

Worker Five: And we need the work.

Worker Six: We'll do it.

They head into the audience to "pick grapes."

Owner: *(watching workers)* They all seem like good workers, but I think I'm going to need some more.

Owner checks the sky or his watch or both.

Owner: It's only midday. I think I'll go back to the market to get some more workers.

Two around Jesus jump up.

Owner: If you guys work in my fields picking grapes from now to sunset, I'll pay you a fair price.

Worker Seven*:* Great. Even though it's pretty hot, I prefer picking grapes to herding sheep.

Worker Eight: Definitely. And I'm tired of standing around the marketplace.

They head into the audience to "pick grapes." They should not exit. They should stay in the audience picking grapes.

Jesus: When he went out about three o'clock, he did the same. And about five o'clock he went out and found others still standing around.

John: This guy doesn't think very far ahead, does he?

Owner: *(to all the remaining still sitting)* You guys are still standing around? Why?

Disciples: What do you mean "why?" / Because you didn't pick us. / That's why.

Owner: What? Am I the only vineyard owner in town?

Disciples: YES!

Owner: Okay. I'll take all of you.

Disciples: GREAT!

Owner: If you guys work in my fields . . .

Worker Nine: We know. We know. Picking grapes . . .

Worker Ten: From now till sunset, which is only an hour . . .

Worker Eleven: You'll pay us a fair wage.

Owner: Right.

Workers Nine, Ten, Eleven: *(together)* Great! We're there!

They head into the audience to pick grapes. All workers reenter.

Worker One: *(to Worker Two)* Would you look at that!

Worker Two: That crazy vineyard owner is bringing on more workers with only an hour of daylight.

Jesus: When evening came, the owner of the vineyard said to his manager,

Owner: Call the laborers in and give them their pay.

The assistant rings a bell and shouts out to workers to come in.

Owner: *(to the assistant, as the workers are walking in)* I want you to pay them starting with the last hired.

Assistant: *(to the owner)* Yes, sir! *(to the workers)* Okay. Everybody who was hired about an hour ago, step forward first. Then those hired three hours ago, and so on.

The group that was hired last steps forward.

Assistant: Here is a denarius for each of you.

Worker Eleven: A whole denarius for one hour's work?

Worker Ten: Are you sure?

Worker Nine: Don't ask him that. Of course he's sure. He knows what he's doing.

Workers One, Two, and Three are at the end of the line.

Worker One: Did you hear that?

Worker Two: He's paying a denarius to the ones who only worked an hour?

Worker Three: That's what he promised us!

Worker One: Yeah. I'll bet he's going to pay us a lot more though, since we worked the whole day. You know, a bonus.

Worker Two: Makes sense to me.

Assistant: *(handing out coins)* One for you. One for you . . .

Workers One, Two, and Three reach the assistant. He hands them each a denarius.

Assistant: Good work, gentlemen. As agreed, here is a denarius for each of you.

Worker Three: Wait a minute.

Worker Two: *(to the owner)* Didn't you give those who worked only an hour a denarius, same as us?

Worker One: That's not fair, is it? We were out there in the hot sun all day.

Owner: But didn't you agree to work all day for one denarius?

Worker One: Yes, but . . .

Owner: And didn't you say at the time that I was being generous with you?

Worker Two: Yes, but . . .

Owner: So, I did you no harm, did I?

Worker Three: Yes, but . . . I mean, no, but . . .

Owner: Don't I have the right to do what I want with my own money?

Workers One, Two, Three: *(together)* Yes, but . . .

Owner: So, you're upset that I am generous with my money? Do you think that's right?

Workers One, Two, Three: *(together)* No, but . . .

Owner: Be happy with what you got. And don't worry about what the others got. You may go. Thank you for your good day's work.

Worker Three: I'm not sure I understand economics.

Worker Two: I sure don't understand his economics.

Worker One: Well, we did get what was promised, I guess.

Worker Three: Yeah. What do you say when somebody is generous with you and even more generous with someone else? That it's not fair?

John: *(to Jesus)* I get it. . . . I think.

Jesus: You will enter the kingdom of heaven through the grace of God alone, through his endless generosity, not through your own efforts. It is God's gift given to those who have faith.

John: Wow! That is generous.

The Ten Bridesmaids

Based on Matthew 25:1–13

Production Notes

Open on Jesus sitting on a rock, teaching a group of disciples and others. As with all of the dramas, the players in the parable would come from the group and can possibly return there instead of exiting.

There is no specific "setting" for where the bridesmaids are gathered.

Speaking Roles
Bartholomew
Peter
Disciples (only as part of group)
Jesus
WB One
WB Two
WB Three
WB Four
WB Five
FB One
FB Two
FB Three
FB Four
FB Five
Servant
Groom

Nonspeaking Roles
Optional: "donkey"
possibly crowd members around Jesus

Note: WB stands for Wise Bridesmaid; **FB** stands for Foolish Bridesmaid

Bridesmaids could be changed to groomsmen or half could be bridesmaids and half groomsmen. However, do not make one sex "wise" and the other "foolish."

Props

flower garlands for bridesmaids' hair, biblical clay lamps for all ten bridesmaids, five cans of oil for wise bridesmaids

Optional: various kinds of modern lamps instead of the clay lamps (use one or the other, not both) and five boxes of light bulbs instead of cans of oil

Bartholomew: Lord, Thomas said he's having trouble understanding the kingdom of heaven, and so—

Peter: *(laughing)* So what else is new? Can Thomas imagine anything that he can't see?

Bartholomew: Well, as I was saying, I'm having a bit of trouble understanding it myself.

Disciples: Yes. / I am too. / Me too. / It's a toughy. / Now it's not really a kingdom, right? / And if it's not here, when is it coming?

Peter: To tell you the truth, Lord, I'm a little fuzzy on it myself.

Jesus: The kingdom of heaven will be like this. Ten bridesmaids took their lamps and went to meet the bridegroom.

Bartholomew: Ten? Wow! I tell you, weddings are getting out of hand these days.

Jesus: Five of them were wise . . .

Disciples around Jesus stand up and move forward to play the parts.

WB One: Ooh. Ooh. I'm wise.

WB Two: Me too. I've even done my homework.

WB Three: I'm wise. I save up for what I buy.

WB Four: I wouldn't be caught dead putting a cart before a horse.

WB Five: I know you're never supposed to count your chickens before they hatch.

Bartholomew: Wow! They sound pretty wise.

Jesus: And five were foolish.

The five foolish bridesmaids aren't paying attention. Suddenly FB One realizes they are supposed to stand up and motions for the others. They all scramble to their feet.

FB One: Don't even ask. I know you're looking at me. Two heads are better than one except when one of them is mine.

FB Two: I get dizzy when I try to see the forest for the trees.

FB Three: I am always parted from my money very quickly.

FB Four: And I always rush in where angels fear to tread.

FB Five: When people pay me a penny for my thoughts, they usually ask for their money back.

Peter: It looks like we have our five foolish bridesmaids.

Jesus: The ten bridesmaids got lamps and went out to wait for the bridegroom . . .

They pick up the lamps that are in a pile on the corner of the stage.

WB One: Where is that groom?

FB One: Maybe he got cold feet.

FB Two: Maybe he didn't get an invitation to the reception.

WB Two: We better get some more oil to keep our lamps burning.

Wise Bridesmaids: Yes. / Oh, good idea. / Good thinking. / Yes, let's . . .

FB Three: Don't be silly. We don't need more oil.

FB Four: Surely the groom will be here before too long.

FB Five: Yes. I thought we were supposed to be the foolish ones.

The five wise bridesmaids each grab a can of oil from side of stage. All ten of them go down into the audience. The wise ones just look out in the distance for the bridegroom. The foolish ones look under chairs and and in corners.

WB Three: What's taking him so long?

WB Four: I don't see him anywhere.

FB One: He's not down there.

FB Two: Maybe he didn't get an invitation to the reception.

WB Five: It's getting cold, but we should wait out here.

WB Four: Let's huddle up for warmth.

They all return to the stage and huddle up. And all fall asleep. For a moment everything is silent. Then a servant enters.

Servant: Hey, wake up! He's here. The bridegroom is here. Wake up!

Bridesmaids: Oh! / Did we fall asleep? / How long have we been out? / Oh my!

Servant: You must go out and greet him!

FB Five: My lamp is low on oil.

FB Three: My lamp is going out!

FB Four: My lamp is out!

FB One: Can you please lend us some of your oil for our lamps?

WB Two: We told you to get oil.

WB One: Why didn't you?

FB Two: Well, who would have thought he'd take so long?

WB Three: We don't have enough for ourselves and you too.

WB Five: If you'd thought of it earlier, you could have bought some.

FB Three: That oil vendor overcharges. It would cost a fortune!

WB One: We just don't have enough. Maybe you can go borrow some. The longer you stand here arguing, the later it will be.

The five foolish bridesmaids wander around the stage searching.

FB One: Didn't there used to be an all-night oil store around here?

FB Two: Yes, I think I know where it is. Follow me.

FB Three: No, I remember, it's been closed for two years. Maybe we can borrow some from my uncle. I think he lives this way.

FB Five: I think we're lost.

FB Four: I can't see.

FB Three: Maybe we should light our lamps so we can see.

The other four foolish bridesmaids just stare at her.

FB Three: Oh yeah. I forgot.

FB One: I think we've ended up where we started.

FB Two: Oh yeah. I just remembered there's an all-night oil store around the corner.

Everyone stares at her.

FB Two: Hey, did I sign up for foolish bridesmaid or not?

The five foolish bridesmaids all exit.

The bridegroom enters with the five wise bridesmaids.

Groom: Thank you, ladies, for waiting for me for so long. And for keeping your lamps lit so that we could find our way.

Wise Bridesmaids: Oh, no problem. / Good to see you. / Happy to do it. / That's what bridesmaids are supposed to do.

Groom: What happened to the other five bridesmaids?

WB One: Well, that's . . . uh . . . a long story.

Groom: Hmm! Well, you can tell me during the feast. Shall we go in?!

They exit.

Jesus: Much later, when the foolish bridesmaids finally got their oil and showed up, the door to the wedding feast was locked.

The foolish bridesmaids enter and knock.

Foolish Bridesmaids: Yoo-hoo! We're here. / Let us in. / We've had a terrible night. / Please! Open the door. / Look. Our lamps are full of oil . . . now.

Groom: *(offstage, behind door or on mike)* Who's there?

FB One: It's the rest of your bridesmaids.

FB Four: Yeah. The foolish ones!

Groom: Do I know you? To tell you the truth, I don't know you at all.

FB Two: *(to the others)* I guess he got his invitation after all.

Groom: Good-bye now.

The foolish bridesmaids walk away, exhausted and disappointed.

FB Three: You know, I bet there's a lesson here.

FB One: Yeah. I wonder what it is?

They exit.